JAMES W. & MICHAL ANN

GOLL

Women on the Front Lines Series

compassion

A
Call
To
Take
Action

DESTINY IMAGE® PUBLISHERS, INC.
P.O. Box 310, Shippensburg, PA 17257-0310

"Speaking to the Purposes of God for this Generation and for the Generations to Come."

This book and all other Destiny Image, Revival Press, Mercy Place, Fresh Bread, Destiny Image Fiction, and Treasure House books are available at Christian bookstores and distributors worldwide.

For a U.S. bookstore nearest you, call **1-800-722-6774.**

For more information on foreign distributors, call **717-532-3040.**

Or reach us on the Internet: **www.destinyimage.com**

ISBN 10: 0-7684-2386-4

ISBN 13: 978-0-7684-2386-0

For Worldwide Distribution, Printed in the U.S.A.

1 2 3 4 5 6 7 8 9 10 11 / 09 08 07 06

DEDICATION

First and foremost, I dedicate this book to Jesus! I've been waiting for many years now, for His promise to me to be fulfilled. In the final days of the angelic visitation I had years ago, I was promised that next time, not only would the angels come, but Jesus Himself would come. I realize that every move of God and every promised visitation is going to look different than we probably think it will be. I'm pondering if Jesus has actually been waiting for me to come where He is. He is in me, with me always, but there's another dimension of experiencing Him—and I believe it's out there, where His Kingdom collides with the systems of the world, and sets things right. Jesus, I want to see You—I want to be where You are. May Your banqueting table be filled, and may we help gather many, many into Your house, that it be full.

To my grandmother, Ann Lucinda McCoy, who charged each one of us grandkids, to always love Jesus, and live for Him every day; who also had a dream in her heart—to be a missionary to China. Grandma—I believe your prayers prepared the path my feet are walking on. Thank you for paving the way for me—with your prayers and with your tears.

I also want to dedicate this book to all the keepers of the flame, those we know, and those who have gone on silently before us, whose history we will learn of when we meet in Heaven. This book is dedicated to the many women who launched out into closed countries to bring the Gospel, and were never heard from again, women compelled to carry the love of Jesus through the very expression of their lives, for some, the only thing they had to give—they gave it all. To the champions of compassion, we honor you.

Michal Ann Goll
Compassion Acts Director
Author, *Call to the Secret Place, Dream Language,
God Encounters, Women on the Front Lines*

ACKNOWLEDGEMENTS

I would like to thank all those who made this project happen. Thank you to Destiny Image, and all the contributing writers. Without each one of you, this project would not have happened. Thank you, Mallory Gabard, James Goll, Lloyd Hildebrand, Julia Loren, Don Milam, Dr. J. Mark Rodgers, and Ada Winn. How wonderful to have a whole company of writers who want to get the message out there.

Thank you to my wonderful husband, James, for your insight into the whole writing process and methodology. Thank you for adding the depth of teaching and instruction you bring to the table. Thank you for your history in missions—driving nails in Guatemala, countless trips to Haiti, train rides and more train rides through Russia, the Ukraine, and trips into Albania. Thank you for sharing your heart with me, and wanting to do this thing called life and ministry—together, each submitting to the other.

Thank you to each one of our wonderful, big-hearted and devoted children, Justin, GraceAnn, Tyler, and Rachel, for bearing with me through the writing deadlines, and encouraging me to go to the ends of the earth to help those less fortunate—to go to the nations armed with the love of Jesus! Thank you for encouraging me to grow and learn and be all God wants me to be. Thank you for believing in me! I love you each so much!

Thank you to our Encounters Network staff, friends, and affiliates for your support and belief in me; and more importantly, belief in God's goodness, the power of love, and the power of one life determined to make a difference.

Thank you, Compassion Acts steering team, Leon Hoover, Dabney Mann, Mark Roye, and Marcus Young, and all those who are partnering with me, and putting your shoulder to the wheel alongside mine.

Thank you to our prayer shield, who continually have lifted me up in prayer, and have been guardians, watching over this little baby, protecting, and giving covering for its release!

Finally and most importantly, oh my dear Jesus—thank you for waking me up, and not letting me stay enclosed in my own little world. Thank you for expanding my vision, my dreams, my goals, and my heart.

ENDORSEMENTS

Compassion is a book about a journey…a journey to which all of us have been called. It will no doubt help men and women alike, as Michal Ann and James have brought wonderful insights, moving personal testimonies, and stories about our heroes of the faith who embraced the same journey. This priceless couple has once again brought us a gem that will help us come into the fullness of Christ.

Bill Johnson
Author, *When Heaven Invades Earth*

When I read through a book, I want more than information (although I love information). I am looking for impartation—something that will change me, transform me. *Compassion, A Call to Take Action* by Michal Ann and James Goll does just that. I passionately pursue more of God's manifest power and glory—why? To fulfill the very mandate expressed in this book. Let's all move forward to fulfill Kingdom mercy and justice in this hour. All of Heaven is cheering us on. Read it!

Patricia King
Extreme Prophetic
Author, *Spiritual Revolution*

Sometimes, one or two quotes from a book can best summarize why the book is so needed. Such is the case when Michal Ann and James Goll tell us that The Salvation Army's originator, William Booth "urged the members of his army to 'try tears' when all else fails.... General Booth shed many tears as they [he and his wife] journeyed together in fulfilling the Father's purposes. Lord Byron once said that the dew of compassion is a tear!" With these quotes, you'll understand why you MUST have this book. Sometimes, compassion isn't just a character trait or a spritual sense within a person. Rather, it is a learned response. I urge you to get this book and LEARN COMPASSION!

Steve Shultz,
The Elijah List www.elijahlist.com
The Voice of the Prophetic Magazine

CONTENTS

PART THREE—LIVING THE CALL

INTRODUCTION

My personal journey leading to the school of compassion started long ago. It began when God touched my life with His amazing love and grace, on the day I was born.

As my mother was giving birth to me, my body was turned around in the breech position. The labor and delivery process began during the early morning hours, so the doctor was not immediately available, though he had been called and was hopefully on the way.

The contractions increased in frequency and the transition came, but still no doctor! I began to emerge from the birth canal, feet first, but my head had not yet appeared. As a result, from the lack of oxygen, my body began to turn blue.

The nurse, who had been there the whole time and had witnessed the entire labor process and the beginning of my delivery, was now faced with a life-or-death decision. She knew the law, which stated that a doctor had to deliver the baby, but she also knew that if she did not do something, I would die from suffocation!

The moment of truth had arrived. Should she follow the requirements of the law or should she act in compassion and save my life? It did not take her long to make this choice, for she put her hand inside the birth canal, found my mouth, put her fingers in my mouth, and pulled me out.

So, I knew the Lord's loving-kindness from the moment of my birth. I was born on February 14—Valentine's Day—and each birthday I celebrate is like receiving a special valentine from my heavenly Father, a personal affirmation which says, "I love you!" Yes, He is full of loving compassion!

Like Christian in *Pilgrim's Progress*, God is taking me on a journey. When I found myself in the valley of intimidation, He introduced me to a "hall of heroes" like the ones described by the prophet Nehemiah and the writer of the Book of Hebrews. (See Nehemiah 7 and Hebrews 11.)

First, He introduced me to many heroines of courage and I was drawn to and immersed in the life of Joan of Arc. She taught me that the darkness of the age we live in does not really matter, because God's light is eternal, and He will open every door for us if we truly love Him and desire for His will to be done. As a result, my heart became a flame of passion that filled me with the courage I needed to sever the chains of intimidation that had held me captive for so long; and my appetite for more of God became truly insatiable!

Next, I began to devour books about other great women of faith and courage: Vibia Perpetua, Sojourner Truth, Harriet Tubman, Aimee Semple McPherson, Lydia Prince, Bertha Smith, Corrie ten Boom, and Jackie Pullinger-To. I wrote about these great women in my book, *Women on the Front Lines, A Call to Courage*, the foundation of my own hall of heroes.

As I built upon that foundation and continued walking through the hallway, the fierier my heart became, and I fell more deeply in love with my heavenly Father, who began helping me to build the second level of my hall of heroes. The Lord gave me fresh insights and showed me how He had always been with me, even during the most trying times of my life. I know that He will always be with me!

Through the writings of Madame Jeanne Guyon I received further spiritual enlightenment and new understandings of God and His ways. Her profound wisdom helped me to firmly establish Jesus as the center of my life; when this happened, everything in my life began to fall into place and I discovered a wonderfully deep peace in Him. This brought great healing and strength to my soul.

As I continued on, I studied the lives of Teresa of Avila, Susanna Wesley, Fanny Crosby, Basilea Schlink, Gwen Shaw, and Elizabeth Alves. Oh, the riches I learned from these special women. Like Susanna Wesley, I determined that my prayer closet would become my apron. I basked in the anointing that rested upon the famous blind hymn writer Fanny Crosby, whose inspiring and stirring hymns ushered in a vital spiritual awakening in her time and continue to minister personally to people everywhere.

These new "friends" of mine were brought together in my second book in the *Women on the Front Lines* series, entitled *A Call to the Secret Place.* This book has released a sweet fragrance of God that I deeply cherish and wish to spread wherever I go.

As a result of all that God has shown me through these experiences and intense study, I am now convinced that, if we have truly experienced the transformation that always occurs when we abide in His presence, it will cause us to turn outward to bring this powerful transformation to the world. After all, this is the power of the love of God that we have known and experienced. His heart is always reaching out to anyone who will receive Him.

If I have truly been set free from fear and intimidation and have been filled with a courageous spirit, and if I have truly found my resting place in the heart of God; I must continue on this journey and move my heart to act in behalf of others. This is something I must embrace, and it requires me to get out of my chair and begin walking with the feet He surely gave me for this purpose. In other words, I must stir myself to action.

Therefore, I've looked into the lives of other women who have known this same compelling call and have forged a trail that we must follow. These trailblazers are Catherine Booth, Nancy Ward, Florence Nightingale, Gladys Aylward, Mother Teresa, Heidi Baker, and a whole company of other women. These ladies have challenged the systems of their day and met life, circumstances, and even governments with attitudes of gutsy determination that flew in the face of and blasted anything that resisted God's love and power.

I love these women. Their don't-tell-me-I-can't determination is what I want for my own life and for your life, as well. With them, I'm committed to continue my journey, and I want to bring as many men and women who desire to love the Lord with all their hearts and to love their neighbors as themselves along with me.

Now I have a few questions for you. What is your heart telling you? Do you want to break open whole regions of the Earth for the Lord's heart? Do you want to make a difference in someone's life? Do you want to break off and break out of the limitations that have bound you up and paralyzed you? Then come along with me. Join me on this exciting journey.

Let's build a whole of company of "laid-down lovers" for Jesus' sake, as Heidi Baker would say. The Father is waiting for us to fill His house! He is waiting and longing for you and me to take action.

Michal Ann Goll
Franklin, Tennessee
August 2006

part one

THE
JOURNEY
BEGINS

This book is a journey into the heart of God. The journey begins with a look at the source of all compassionate action—God's compassionate heart. You will discover that our compassion is a reflection of the All Compassionate One. John writes, *"He who does not love has not become acquainted with God, for God is love"* (1 John 4:8). Our love, replicated in our actions toward others, is a reflection of the depth of our relationship with God.

Yes, God is love, and the essence of His being is manifested in His acts toward us. His conduct toward people reveals His compassion for people. Those who bear His nature will also reflect His character in their actions in the human city. He longs for us to become love and compassion in the midst of a world starving for just a little love. In order to do so, however, we must get to know Him intimately and personally, as Jesus did. We must be connected to the Source and allow His love to flow through us. As that love begins to freely flow to us from our Father it will eventually flow through us to others in loving words and compassionate acts.

In this first section you will learn what compassion is, how God's compassion works, and the power of tears. You will also learn about a great model of compassion, the cofounder of the Salvation Army—Catherine Booth. You will discover that love is more than a concept. The word must be translated into emotion and exploit.

It was Catherine's husband, William Booth, who urged the members of his army to "try tears," when all else failed, and she and General Booth shed many tears as they journeyed together in fulfilling the Father's purposes. Lord Byron once said that the dew of compassion is a tear...and so it is.

Similarly, Jesus frequently wept when He saw the needs of the people and was moved with compassion to do something about them. He sowed in tears and reaped in joy, and you can do the same, for His power and anointing rest upon you.

Like William and Catherine Booth, as a husband-and-wife team, we must unite our hearts to go forth in compassion to the world. We realize, though, that we still have a lot to learn about converting desire into deed. In many ways our journey has just begun.

Each step of the way, however, we have learned to look to Jesus, who truly is the personification of compassion. The lives of those who have gone before us will also serve as a source of great inspiration. They will encourage us to reshape our world as they reshaped their world by the love of God.

Our prayer for you: "...*that He may grant you a spirit of wisdom and revelation [of insight into mysteries and secrets] in the [deep and intimate] knowledge of Him, by having the eyes of your heart flooded with light, so that you can know and understand the hope to which He has called you, and how rich is His glorious inheritance in the saints (His set-apart ones), and [so that you can know and understand] what is the immeasurable and unlimited and surpassing greatness of His power in and for us who believe, as demonstrated in the working of His mighty strength*" (Eph. 1:17-19).

So, let the journey begin!

chapter one

God's Heart of Compassion

by

Michal Ann Goll

*He has showed you, O man, what is good. And what does the Lord
require of you but to do justly, and to love kindness and mercy, and
to humble yourself and walk humbly with your God?* (Micah 6:8)

WILL YOU JOIN ME?

Over the past several years I've been on a personal journey of amazing breadth and depth. I must have more of Jesus, and I am determined to know Him more fully than I've ever known Him before. I want to take you on this journey with me. Will you join me?

Certainly, I have loved the Lord for as long as I can remember. Through the years He has been wooing me and drawing me deeper and deeper into His heart. Like a tractor beam, His gaze has utterly captured me. As in any relationship, if I want more of Him, I must give Him more of me.

This may sound simple, but the ramifications run a deep course through my innermost being and form my life's very destiny. I must learn to walk, talk, and live as Jesus did and as He continues to do. This is my journey—a journey into the heart of God, where I will and must learn His ways.

YOU HAVE TO BE AVAILABLE

On a recent trip to Thailand I found myself sitting in a Mexican restaurant in Bangkok. The young ladies who worked as servers were wearing cowboy hats, cowboy boots, and other western wear. I thought it was really funny to see such outfits in Bangkok, never mind a Mexican restaurant!

I'd been in Thailand for a couple of weeks and had eaten a variety of dishes, some of which caused me to wonder about their ingredients, and I was gaining a little skill in eating with chopsticks. This Mexican restaurant represented my first opportunity to taste home foods and flavors with which I was more familiar.

My friends and I were having a delightful conversation—a nice respite from our hectic schedule of prayer meetings, travel, sleeping in different hotels, and many, many meetings. As I looked around the room and through the front window, I noticed a young man who was standing outside. He was holding a sign, and he had several little toys dangling on fine strings all around him.

From the booth where we were sitting, I noticed his sign read that he was deaf and he had created these little toys, which were crickets, out of bits of bamboo. He was selling them for a modest price of 20 baht (approximately 50 cents) apiece, so he could buy food.

Though he was a simple and needy young man, he didn't look like he was begging. He stood upright, showed no emotion, and did not really try to sell me anything. He did not have the typical pleading eyes of a beggar, and he did not gesture for my attention.

I was impressed by how he stood with an air of quiet self-respect and seeming uprightness of heart. I will never forget the look I saw in his eyes. We did not exchange a word between us, but our hearts touched each other that day as we peered into each other's souls. I believe I gave him something that day—something far more than the 20 baht it cost me to buy a cricket. I gave him my promise to do all I could with my life, to make a difference in his life and in the lives of others like him.

At the same time, he gave me something, something I desperately needed. He gave me the privilege of touching his life, of making a difference. I caught a glimpse into the heart of God. This young man showed me that you don't have to be somebody who is important or famous; you just have to be available. You have to be willing to engage in the journey and walk the path that Jesus walks every day. This is what the journey of learning God's ways is all about.

Whenever I look at my little cricket I bought from this young man, I remember this treasured experience, and I renew my commitment to the Lord Jesus Christ. Thus, I continue on the journey that has been set before me.

Do you want more of Jesus? Is your heart engaged with the things that move His heart? Do you want more of the Father's love deposited in your heart? How can we understand this amazing love that He so deeply desires for us to experience? His love is beyond our mental abilities to comprehend. Many of us have tainted understandings of what a father is like. Our understanding of fatherhood is shaped by our childhood experiences with our earthly fathers. So, we have to ask ourselves, "What do I really know about God and His heart? What do I really know about His mercy and compassion?" To know His mercy and compassion, we must open our hearts to Him. We must go to the place where He exposes the tenderness of His heart—into the written Word.

ACT JUSTLY AND LOVE MERCY

In the book *The Justice God Is Seeking*, the author and our friend David Ruis writes, "Steeped in humility, we are called to act justly and to love mercy. Don't miss this! Justice is an *action*, to be done in and through the power of Christian community, *but mercy is to be loved*. It is not an action; it is a passion."[1]

True compassion and mercy stem from a passion for the Father's heart. Do you love mercy? When we learn to truly love mercy and compassion, out of our passion for God's heart, we will be motivated to act justly.

Justice and righteousness form the foundation of the Father's throne. The psalmist writes, *"Righteousness and justice are the foundation of Your throne: mercy and loving-kindness and truth go before Your face"* (Ps. 89:14).

Go to God's throne of grace as we begin and ask Him for a grace of impartation and a spirit of revelation to come upon you. Ask God to enlighten your mind and to fill your heart with His fire. Open your heart to the Holy Spirit and let Him speak to you, guide you, teach you, and move you. Let the river of God, which is always full, flow forth in all its energy and power.

The writer of the Book of Hebrews says, *"Let us then fearlessly and confidently and boldly draw near to the throne of grace (the throne of God's unmerited favor to us sinners), that we may receive mercy [for our failures] and find grace to help in good time for every need [appropriate help and well-timed help, coming just when we need it]"* (Heb. 4:16).

CONSIDER THE WEAK AND THE POOR

Did you ever consider the fact that happiness comes from walking in compassion? This is what David meant when he wrote, *"Blessed (happy, fortunate, to be envied) is he who considers the weak and the poor: the Lord will deliver him in the time of evil and trouble"* (Ps. 41:1). What a glorious promise this is!

The psalmist then goes on to list some of the other benefits to be derived from considering the weak and the poor (see Psalm 41:1-4):

The Lord will protect us.

The Lord will keep us alive.

We shall be called "blessed in the land."

We will not be given over to our enemies.

The Lord will sustain us.

The Lord will refresh us.

The Lord will strengthen us.

The Lord will turn, change, and transform us.

These are just some of the things that happen when we are filled with compassion and reach out in love to others. Doesn't this make you want to really be in tune with God's heart as you begin your journey?

GOD'S HEART OF COMPASSION

God's compassions never fail. In fact, they are renewed every day. (See Lamentations 3:22.) He wants us to keep our hearts open to Him each day, as well.

We must be careful to guard against any bitterness or hardness of heart that may try to creep into our lives. God actually commands us to never let our hearts and minds grow hard or cold:

> *If there is among you a poor man, one of your kinsmen in any of the towns of your land which the Lord your God gives you, you shall not harden your [minds and] hearts or close your hands to your poor brother. But you shall open your hands wide to him and shall surely lend him sufficient for his need in whatever he lacks. Beware lest there be a base thought in your [minds and] hearts, and you say, The seventh year, the year of release, is at hand, and your eye be evil against your poor brother and you give him nothing, and he cry to the Lord against you, and it be sin in you. You shall give to him freely without begrudging it; because of this the Lord will bless you in all your work and in all you undertake* (Deuteronomy 15:7-10).

What does God want from us? Open hands and open hearts and a willingness to help those in need. He wants us to give freely and cheerfully. This is mercy in action, the love of God reaching out to the oppressed.

This passage refers to the seventh year—the year of Jubilee—when all the lands would lay fallow and the slaves would be set free. He warns the people against looking to the seventh year as the time when their needs would be met instead of getting involved in the here-and-now. In fact, God calls such a consideration "a base thought," something that actually leads to sin.

Notice how God tells us to open our hands wide to the needy and the poor in *"your land."* What is your land? Everyone will have a different answer, depending on the work of God in their hearts. But this we know, "our land" is local, it's home. We are to start at home, but not stop there. We must enlarge our hearts, and do all we can to reach the peoples of every nation, tribe, and tongue.

TRUE JUSTICE

True justice involves both kindness and compassion. Zechariah writes, *"Thus has the Lord of hosts spoken: Execute true judgment and show mercy and kindness and tender compassion, every man to his brother; and oppress not the widow or the fatherless, the temporary resident or the poor, and let none of you devise or imagine or think evil against his brother in your heart"* (Zech. 7:9-10).

Do you see the relationship between justice and compassion that is portrayed here? In order to understand God's plumb line of justice we have to know what He values. On a recent trip to Mozambique the Lord showed me something I had never seen before, and, as He did so, He said to me, *"Mercy without justice enables thievery!"*

This helped me to understand that our concept of mercy and compassion is limited. In fact, many times it is askew. All too often people think that mercy, simply stated, is pity. Though pity is certainly an element of mercy, true mercy and compassion involve so much more.

God always acts from both justice and mercy, and you really can't have one without the other. Sometimes the most merciful thing is to say no to someone who is seeking something from you, particularly if you are looking at the person's stated need through the eyes of both justice and mercy.

The boundaries of the field of mercy and compassion must be firmly established and clearly delineated. We don't ever want anything to encroach on territory that belongs to the Lord, and is set apart for the poor and needy.

While I was in Mozambique one time, I observed some children who were beggars from a village nearby. There are many needy children there, as disease, war, poverty, and drought have ravaged the land and torn families apart. Many children have no parents; as they have died from AIDS, or other causes. Many children beg, but some have learned how to "work the system."

In a church service one Sunday morning, a few boys entered the tent (sanctuary) for the sole purpose of seeing what they could get from people. They could spot the new visitors. These unsuspecting people gathered these young boys in their arms, not engaging in spiritual discernment. They just wanted to bless some of these children.

The problem was that this particular group of boys was looking for things they could steal and sell later. They worked their plan, playing the part and got into camera cases and people's bags. While one would occupy the person, one or two others would look for what they could steal. As I watched this situation unfolding, I began to understand that some of them were actually operating out of demonic activity in order to get what they could from people.

This is where discernment comes into play. We need to be sure that the one in front of us has a genuine need before we attempt to respond to that need. Did the boys have a legitimate need? Yes. As food was always served there, they had the opportunity to fill their stomachs. But what was the condition of the hearts? They also had the opportunity to know Jesus; but they were on a different mission. They were in church to steal. The attention that was given to those boys denied other dear children who really could have used that love, those hugs, that attention. The children who were really needy, with open loving hearts to the Lord, suffered because of the others' thievery.

Here's another story. One man who was with us had brought several deflated soccer balls to Mozambique, because he knew the children there rarely get to see one. One boy came up to him and began begging for money. The man gave him a soccer ball instead. A little bit later, the boy returned. He had ruined the ball, and he began to demand money in exchange for it! Even if he couldn't use the ball, or didn't want it, he had no concept of giving it away to someone else. His mind was consumed with the love of money. This was true thievery! The boy had destroyed the ball so nobody else could enjoy it!

We need to understand what mercy and compassion are according to God's standards, not according to the standards of secular humanism. From His point of view, compassion must always involve justice.

So, let's continue looking at God's heart as it is revealed in the Bible.

GOD'S HEART CONCERNING BLESSING

In the Book of Job, we read:

When I went out to the gate of the city, when I prepared my seat in the street [the broad place for the council at the city's gate], the young men saw me and hid themselves: the aged rose up and stood. The princes refrained from talking and laid their hands on their mouths; the voices of the nobles were hushed, and their tongues cleaved to the roof of their mouths. For when the ear heard, it called me happy and blessed me; and when the eye saw, it testified for me [approvingly], because I delivered the poor who cried, the fatherless and him who had none to help him. The blessing of him who was about to perish came upon me, and I caused the widow's heart to sing for joy. I put on righteousness, and it clothed me or clothed itself with me; my justice was like robe and a turban or a diadem or a crown! I was eyes to the blind, and feet was I to the lame. I was a father to the poor and needy; the cause of him I did not know I searched out. And I broke the jaws or the big teeth of the unrighteous and plucked the prey out of his mouth (Job 29:7-17).

I love this passage, for it shows what God's mercy and compassion are like, and it reveals how He wants us to live. Are you ready to deliver the poor and become a parent to the fatherless? Are you willing to be the eyes of the blind and the feet of the lame? Do you want to cause the widow's heart to sing for joy? How far are you willing to go in searching out the needs of those you do not know?

God wants to bless you as you reach out to all these people and those who are about to perish. Clothe yourself with His righteousness and let His justice be your robe and your crown. Confront the enemy with the power God has invested in you.

TRUE JUDICIAL GOVERNMENT

God wants governments to rule with justice, righteousness, and compassion, but we all know that this is not always the case. The psalmist writes, *"God stands in the assembly [of the representatives] of God; in the midst of the magistrates or judges He gives judgment.... How long will you [magistrates or judges] judge unjustly and show partiality to the wicked? ...Do justice to the weak (poor) and fatherless; maintain the rights of the afflicted and needy. Deliver the poor and needy; rescue them out of the hand of the wicked"* (Ps. 82:1-4).

Here we see God's heart concerning true judicial government. Such a government should not show partiality, and it should always do justice to the poor, the fatherless, the afflicted, and the needy. In fact, it should even deliver the poor and needy and rescue them from the wicked.

As followers of Jesus, we should do everything within our power to make sure that this is the kind of government we have. We should vote for godly candidates, and we should vote the wicked out of office. God might even call us to run for public office ourselves so that His justice, righteousness, and mercy can take hold where we live. It is time to stand up in the seats of government and let our lights shine!

GOD'S HEART CONCERNING HONOR

The following Scripture shook me to the core of my being as its truth penetrated my spirit: *"He who oppresses the poor reproaches, mocks, and insults his Maker, but he who is kind and merciful to the needy honors Him"* (Prov. 14:31). I don't know how this could be any clearer.

Do you want to honor God? If your answer is yes, you must operate in kindness and mercy to the needy. To do otherwise brings reproach, mockery, and insult to God!

GOD'S HEART CONCERNING LENDING

In Proverbs 19 we read, *"He who has pity on the poor lends to the Lord, and that which he has given He will repay to him"* (Prov. 19:17).

This reminds me of what Jesus said, *"...Truly I tell you, in so far as you did it for one of the least [in the estimation of men] of these My brethren, you did it for Me"* (Matt. 25:40).

What you give to the poor, you give to God, and He promises to repay you!

GOD'S HEART CONCERNING RIGHTEOUSNESS

God wants our righteousness to be consistent, as the following verse from Proverbs shows: *"The [consistently] righteous man knows and cares for the rights of the poor, but the wicked man has no interest in such knowledge"* (Prov. 29:7).

Look at the contrast that is painted for us here. Whereas the righteous person *knows* and *cares* for the rights of the poor, the wicked person is completely uninterested in such knowledge and activity.

I would like to think of myself as a righteous person, but there have been many, many times when I've had to repent of my lack of mercy and my unwillingness to tune my heart to God's heart.

My desire is to be like the woman who is described in Proverbs 31: *"She opens her hand to the poor, yes, she reaches out her filled hands to the needy [whether in body, mind, or spirit] (Prov. 31:20).* This verse speaks volumes to me, for it shows a righteous woman in action.

GOD'S CHOSEN FAST

A few years ago I had a dream in which I saw 20 or 30 people standing all around me. It seemed that they had been witnesses of my life. One particular man who was standing over me had a spirit of prophecy resting on him. He reminded me of an old-fashioned water pump, the kind where you prime the pump first and then start moving the handle up and down. I sensed that, as this man moved from side to side, the water of God's Word was building up inside of him.

In this dream I was very sick. My body was crumpled over an old stone wall, and I was crying, "Will someone get me a doctor? I'm very, very sick!"

Everybody stared at me, and the man I mentioned said, "Don't you know you've been called to prayer and fasting?"

I said, "I need help. Will someone please get me a doctor?"

Again, he said, "Don't you know you've been called to prayer and fasting?"

I whimpered, "Please! Somebody help me! Please! I need help!"

The man stood in front of me and repeated, "Don't you know you've been called to prayer and fasting?" Then he added: "Don't you know that if you would enter into prayer and fasting, you would extend the orphan's bread from three to five days?"

This question hit me hard. I began to see that what I needed was not a doctor after all. What I really needed was to obey the Lord by entering into a place of prayer and fasting.

I'm terrible at fasting. I really am. Fasting represents a monumental struggle with my flesh. I really have a hard time with it. God's chosen fast, however, goes beyond the issue of food and flesh; it goes deep into your heart.

God's chosen fast becomes a lifestyle that we are called to embrace. What is His chosen fast? The Bible tells us, *"[Rather] is not this the fast that I have chosen: to loose the bonds of wickedness, to undo the bands of the yoke, to let the oppressed go free, and that you break every [enslaving] yoke?"* (Isa. 58:6). Now that's a powerful fast!

Have you entered a fast that divides your bread with the hungry? Have you brought the homeless into your home, covered the naked, and provided for the needs of your family and all those around you? (See Isaiah 58:7.)

This is God's chosen fast, and it is truly an exciting fast in which to get engaged, for this is always its result:

> *Then shall your light break forth like the morning, and your healing (your restoration and the power of a new life) shall spring forth speedily; your righteousness (your rightness, your justice, and your right relationship with God) shall go before you (conducting you to peace and prosperity], and the glory of the Lord shall be your rear guard* (Isaiah 58:8).

I don't know about you, but I'll sure take that. This is God's chosen fast for you and me.

THE COMPASSION OF JESUS

David Ruis writes, "As followers of Jesus, we cannot ignore what moved Him to send out the first of His disciples, what moves Him still to send us out today; *compassion*. Biblical compassion is a uniquely Christian virtue."[2]

Jesus always *saw* the need first, then He was *moved* with a compassion so strong that it always led Him to *do* something in response to the need. Matthew writes, *"When He saw the throngs, He was moved with pity and sympathy for them, because they were bewildered (harassed and distressed and dejected and helpless), like sheep without a shepherd"* (Matt. 9:36).

He then went on to tell His disciples to pray that God would send laborers into His harvest. We need to engage in the same kind of prayer today, for so many people are confused like sheep without a shepherd. God is looking for people who will go out into the fields that are now white unto harvest. (See Matthew 9:37-38.)

The Greek word for compassion (pity and sympathy) that is used here is *splanchnizomai*, and it means to be moved deep within. It involves a sense of yearning in behalf of others.

If you have compassion, you will be moved to take action, as Jesus always was and is. God wants you to know His compassion, receive His compassion, live His compassion, and share His compassion with others.[3]

All the Scriptures within this chapter open God's heart to you. He is your loving heavenly Father, and He wants you to share in His compassion.

I agree with David Ruis, who writes, "To touch Christ is to touch compassion. Far beyond a guilt-trip, a tweaked conscience or a pale sense of pity, compassion reaches into the very guts and demands action. It compels prayers that will move heaven, intercessions that cry out for workers to be thrust into this weighted-down harvest. It motivates one to move—to go and set it right—to administer justice through the power of the Kingdom."[4]

Compassion will move so deeply within your being that many times you will find yourself moved to the point of tears and agony. Ah, this is a beautiful place. God places great value in your tears, and as we turn to the next chapter, you will discover this is a deep well which moves Heaven on behalf of others.

Heavenly Father, we come to you right now in the name of Jesus. We ask you to light the fire of passion in our lives and let it become the kind of compassion that doesn't just look at the need, but looks to you. Help us to become so passionate for loving you and knowing your heart that we will move in compassion to all those in need. We ask that you will bring about a corporate shift of thinking and acting in the entire Body of Christ, that your people would become passionate about compassion by being passionate for you. We cry out to you, Father, and ask that you would take the Scriptures we've read and discussed in this chapter and drop their truths deep within our hearts. Let your Word continue to flow within the depths of our spirits so we will be able to receive all the spiritual nutrients you have for us. Drop your plumb line of justice through all of our thoughts and feelings, all of our traditions and training, and let us learn to do justly and to love mercy and to walk humbly with you. In Jesus' name, Amen.

ENDNOTES

1. David Ruis, *The Justice God Is Seeking* (Regal Books: Ventura, CA, 2006), 80.

2. Ibid., 10.

3. Charles H. Spurgeon, "The Compassion of Jesus," a sermon he delivered on December 24, 1914, at the Metropolitan Tabernacle, Newington, England.

4. David Ruis, *Justice God Is Seeking.*

chapter two

The Compassionate Power of Tears
by
James W. Goll

And as He approached, He saw the city, and He wept [audibly]
over it. Exclaiming, would that you had known personally, even at
least in this your day, the things that make for peace.... But now
they are hidden from your eyes (Luke 19:41-42).

Look, Listen, and Obey

Jesus frequently used the word "behold" when He was teaching His
disciples the truths about His Kingdom. In so doing He was telling
them to open their spiritual eyes and see the truth He was conveying.

When Jesus saw the throngs of people who were suffering as a
result of their sins, He was moved with compassion for them. Often, He
even wept over them. The shortest verse in the Bible says, *"Jesus wept"*
(John 11:35). What was He weeping over here? First, He saw the need,
which was the death of Lazarus.

Then He heard the cry of Martha's heart: *"Master, if You had been*
here, my brother would not have died" (John 11:21). At this point Martha
expressed her faith in the Master's ability to heal. She said, *"I know that*
whatever You ask from God, He will grant it to You" (John 11:22).

Next, Jesus heard the piercing cries of Mary, the sister of Martha and Lazarus, and *"When Jesus saw her sobbing, and the Jews who came with her [also] sobbing, He was deeply moved in spirit and troubled..."* (John 11:33).

Because He saw and listened actively to the heart cries of Martha, Mary, and the assembled Jews, and was tuned in to the resonance of the heart of Father God Himself, Jesus was *moved with compassion,* and in turn ministered effectively to the urgent need at hand. John the beloved describes in detail how Lazarus came forth from the tomb; he bolted forth demonstrating the power of the resurrection from the dead! Tears preceded this power encounter. Perhaps compassion and power are inevitably linked.

Yes, our tears have the power to cleanse, to enable us to see, and to thrust us to action in behalf of those in need.

As we hear God speaking to our hearts, we need to obey His inner promptings. As good parents raising their children frequently say, "Just listen and obey!" Obedience brings action to our feelings. Obedience demonstrates commitment to our inner convictions and moves us beyond ourselves.

BOWELS OF MERCY

Jesus was frequently moved with pity, sympathy, and compassion for the people He saw around Him. He really saw them, and He saw their needs. This means He was fully aware, perceptive, understanding, and responsive to them.

Often, the Lord saw people as being bewildered, like sheep without a shepherd, and this deeply troubled Him, as we see in the Gospel of Mark: *"As Jesus landed, He saw a crowd waiting, and He was moved with compassion for them, because they were like sheep without a shepherd: and He began to teach them many things"* (Mark 6:34).

It has been accurately said that when a need is presented to us we really have three options:

- To be inactive—to do nothing. Like the proverbial ostrich, we can choose to stick our heads in the sand and hope the problem will go away.

- To be reactive—this is an emotional response, usually in the form of anger—to a troubling situation.

- To be proactive—this involves taking positive steps to rectify the problem.

Jesus, when He was moved with compassion, was always proactive. In the case just cited in the Scripture, we see that He responded to the disorientation He saw in the people by commanding Kingdom order and thus teaching them to rule and reign in life.

As we go forth in compassion, we need to do more than just express sympathy or pity. As Jesus did, we need *to do* something concrete to help others. Perhaps the best help we can give others is to teach them how to overcome through faith, prayer, and spiritual understanding. We need to exemplify Kingdom authority right out in the open as Jesus did for all to see. The kind of compassion Jesus walked in was not weak and passive—it was tender yet tough, sensitive yet confrontational.

Jesus' heart was and is yet to this day, filled with compassion. Jesus modeled compassionate living in personal ways for both individuals and for the masses. He practiced what Paul preached,

> *Clothe yourselves therefore, as God's own chosen ones (His own picked representatives), [who are] purified and holy and well-beloved [by God Himself, by putting on behavior marked by] tenderhearted pity and mercy, kind feeling, a lowly opinion of yourselves, gentle ways, [and] patience [which is tireless and long-suffering, and has the power to endure whatever comes, with good temper]. Be gentle and forbearing with one another and, if one has a difference (a grievance or complaint) against another, readily pardoning each other; even as the Lord has [freely] forgiven you, so must you also [forgive]* (Colossians 3:12-13).

Can there be any more vivid portrayal of compassion than this? This is a verbal picture of what God expects from each of us. It is the "bowels of mercy" that the King James Version of the Bible tells us to "put on."

The bowels are found deep within us, and the fountain of tears that flows when our hearts are filled with mercy comes from deep within our spirits, where the Holy Spirit, who groans in compassion with *"unspeakable yearnings and groanings too deep for utterance,"* resides. (See Romans 8:26.)

So, listen and obey. Let compassion flow forth from your inner most being—your bowels of mercy. Remember, it is out of practicing His presence that compassion is born. The love of God works inward (within you), but, as it works inward, it always begins to move outward.

SEVEN DOORS

One evening while my friend Marcus Young of Divine Inheritance and I were waiting on the Lord together, I received a remarkable spiritual vision of seven consecutive doors. I tell of this vision in full in my book *The Lost Art of Practicing His Presence*. But for right now, let me simply give you an overview of that God encounter.

I saw in the spirit a succession of seven doorways and over each one there was a word written. The word "Forgiveness" was engraved over the first door. As I crossed over the threshold of that first door, I was able to see what was written over the second door: "Cleansed by the Blood."

This experience helped me to understand that there is a place in our walk with God where, though we know we are forgiven, we might not have fully realized or experienced the reality of total cleansing through the blood of Jesus Christ. As I passed through the second doorway, I experienced the cleansing power of the blood in a new and total way. I knew I was truly cleansed by His blood.

I went on through the third and fourth doorways; they dealt with areas of holiness and sanctification through the power of the Holy Spirit. Then I came to the fifth doorway and noticed that its title was "Grace." As I walked through that portal, a new revelation of the grace of God came upon me.

I learned much as I continued in this interactive vision. I discovered that grace empowers the believer with the anointing and I also learned that all of God's giftings are all received by grace. These are what I call "gracelets," little drops of grace.

From that phenomenal experience I learned that the degree of anointing one has comes from passing through God's doorway to grace. It is then that the oil of the Holy Spirit begins to fall on us.

The word "Mercy" was prominently displayed over the sixth doorway. Whereas grace had dealt with God's action toward me, I now learned that mercy had to do with our actions toward others.

This was a very long passageway, but at its end I could make out what was written over the seventh door: "Union With Christ." I wanted so desperately to get to the seventh door, but I knew I couldn't do so until I had completely passed through the sixth corridor—the realm of mercy. This realization filled my heart with anguish.

All I could do was cry, "Lord, teach me your mercy," for I knew then that the only way I would ever be able to enjoy complete union with Christ would be by walking in mercy and compassion at all times.

SYMPATHETIC CONSCIOUSNESS

Compassion involves a sympathetic consciousness toward others. More simply stated, it is being stricken in your heart with a sensitive spiritual awareness of others' hurts, positions, distresses, and dilemmas. More than that, it involves having a divine motivation to do something about their situation.

The following verse gives us insight into the heart of compassion at work: "Brethren, if any person is overtaken in misconduct or sin of any sort, you who are spiritual [who are responsive to and controlled by the Spirit] should set him right and restore and reinstate him, without any sense of superiority and with all gentleness..." (Gal. 6:1).

The Lord Jesus has a heart of compassion toward each one of us, as we see in Hebrews 4:15: *"For we do not have a High Priest Who is unable to understand and sympathize and have a shared feeling with our weaknesses and infirmities and liability to the assaults of temptation, but One Who has been tempted in every respect as we are, yet without sinning"* (Heb. 4:15).

Jesus knows about our struggles. He shares our feelings and bears our burdens with us. He truly understands what we are going through.

It is this knowledge that enables us to: *"...fearlessly and confidently and boldly draw near to the throne of grace (the throne of God's unmerited favor to us sinners), that we may receive mercy [for our failures] and find grace to help in good time for every need [appropriate help and well-timed help, coming just when we need it]"* (Heb. 4:16).

We really do have a High Priest who sympathizes with us and gives us His mercy! He is our compassionate Lord and Savior. The psalmist puts it this way: *"The Lord is good to all, and His tender mercies are over all His works [the entirety of things created]"* (Ps. 145:9).

The Lord is good to *all*, and His compassion extends to everything and *everyone* He has created.

HIS COMPASSIONS FAIL NOT

Jeremiah wrote, *"It is because of the Lord's mercy and loving-kindness that we are not consumed, because His [tender] compassions fail not. They are new every morning; great and abundant is Your stability and faithfulness"* (Lam. 3:22-23).

These verses give us a clear understanding of the heart of our Father and the way He deals with His children. The late John Wimber shared a revealing testimony in his outstanding book, *Power Healing*.[1] One day, as he was praying, he was discussing an observation with the Lord about how many people, including himself, are sometimes afraid to pray for the sick.

As he contemplated this idea, he began to understand that this may well be due to the fact that many do not understand God's nature and how He works. Then the Lord spoke to John and told him that most people are hesitant and even fearful about praying for another's healing because they misunderstand His compassion and mercy. The Lord told him that many know about Him but they do not really *know Him*.

This word from the Lord empowered John to go forth in faith and compassion and, as a result, God used him as a vehicle through which His healing mercies flowed, but his joy was tempered somewhat when he received a rather disturbing vision from the Lord.

As he was driving, he saw what looked like a cloud bank over the sky. When this vision came before him, he pulled his car to the side of the road. Then he realized it wasn't a cloud that he saw after all; it was a honeycomb filled with honey, and it was dripping on the people below.

Some people eagerly gulped down the honey, loving its sweet taste and offering it to others. Other people, however, were irritated by the sticky honey that was being poured all over them, so they tried to wipe it off and complained about "the mess."

The Lord explained to John that the honey was His mercy, which to some is a blessing and to others is a hindrance. He told John that there was plenty for everyone and that we shouldn't beg Him for healing, because the problem isn't on His end; it is with the people.

Like Jesus, we need to weep over the people who are wandering like sheep without a shepherd. Often they just do not understand who God is, what He has already accomplished on Calvary and what He wants to do for them. Some of you know that my wife and I have both had severe bouts with cancer. But this we know, and from this position we fight— God is good *all* the time! Yes, His mercy endures forever!

TRY TEARS

General William Booth, who founded the Salvation Army with his wife, Catherine, received several letters from people who were lamenting over the seeming lack of progress in their ministries. In their letters they expressed little hope about saving the lost. They said that things were too hard and that it appeared as if nothing was happening.

Booth's response to them was very simple. He tore off a piece of a brown paper sack, wrote a note on it, and sent it to the seekers. It poignantly stated: "Try tears."[2]

We need to let our hearts be broken with the things that break the heart of God. One pastor put it this way, "My church will never grow while my eyes are dry."

What a splendid way this is of expressing the flaming burden that comes when our hearts are broken before God. Basilea M. Schlinck wrote, "The first characteristic of the kingdom of heaven is the overflowing joy that comes from contrition and repentance, tears of contrition soften even the hardest hearts."[3]

Tears of contrition come from our brokenness before God. They express our utter abhorrence of our sinfulness and our complete dependence upon the Lord for everything. David Brainerd, the well-known missionary to the Indians of North America, recorded the following entry in his diary on October 18, 1780: "My soul was exceedingly melted and bitterly mourned over my exceeding sinfulness and vileness. I never before felt so pungent and deep a sense of the odious nature of sin as at this time. My soul was then carried forth and loved to God and had a lively sense of God's love to me."[4]

This was an experience that Brainerd had as he was praying while standing in the snow on a bitter winter day. He was smitten with a great revelation of His utter dependence upon and absolute need for God, and he saw his own sinfulness in a new light. But God didn't leave him there; He gave him a greater revelation of Himself and His great love for him.

THE PRAYER OF TEARS

Compassionate praying, as David Brainerd's experience shows, is prophetic praying. It deals with the deep-seated desires of the spirit, a craving for that which does not presently exist. It is deep calling unto deep. (See Psalm 42:7.) This involves profound yearning, crying, groaning, longing, and earnestness that come from deep within you. It is the beginning of the prayer of tears.

The prayer of tears is a form of compassion in action. It works in an intercessory and prophetic fashion, touching the lives of those we pray for. As we engage in compassionate praying, God puts His heart within us. We actually receive an impartation of something that is not of ourselves, and we are moved with tenderness, sensitivity, and mercy. This allows us to actually feel the pain of another person at least for a while. We could say that this is the "gift of pain," a gift in the sense that it is a supernatural impartation of compassion, the ability to suffer with those who suffer. (See 1 Corinthians 12:26.)

A few years ago, when my dear brother Mahesh Chavda was praying for me, as I lay prostrate on the floor, the Holy Spirit began to speak to me. He said, *"I am going to give you the gift of pain."*

Now, this was a message that I wasn't too sure about, as you can well imagine. The Holy Spirit went on, *"I'm going to give you the gift of pain, and you will feel my feelings temporarily in your being, your body."*

The word "temporarily" helped to ease my anxiety over this message a little bit. It was then that an entirely new spiritual understanding came to me. I began to realize that it is possible to feel the sufferings of others for a while when we are interceding for them. I think what happens is that God actually puts His heart, which breaks with compassion for others, within us for a while so that we will be truly able to bear their burdens before His throne.

As you wait before the Lord and give Him your heart, He will touch you with a portion of His burden and give you His heart to enable you to carry others at least for a while before His throne. When this happens, it's as if you become a little donkey—a beast of burden—for Him. In this way God puts His burden upon you.

The Holy Spirit concluded what He was saying to me with this sentence: *"I'm going to give you the gift of pain, and you will feel the fellowship of My sufferings, and you will feel the pains of others, and then, as you release this and bring it back to Me, the pain will lift."*

Then I realized how glorious it is to be smitten with the things that break God's heart. Indeed, it's one of the greatest privileges we could ever have. To think that God in all of His glory and grandeur would share His heart with us and give us His pain is mind-boggling. It truly is an honor to be a donkey for Him!

In fact, one time after hearing me speak, someone made me a T-Shirt and sent it to me. It bolded stated, "I'm a jackass for Jesus!" Yes, I resemble that! How about you?

THE FELLOWSHIP OF HIS SUFFERINGS

Paul writes,

[For my determined purpose is] that I may know Him [that I may progressively become more deeply and intimately acquainted with Him, perceiving and recognizing and understanding the wonders of His Person more strongly and more clearly], and that I may in that same way come to know the power outflowing from His resurrection [which it exerts over believers], and that I may share His sufferings as to be continually transformed [in spirit into His likeness even] to His death (Philippians 3:10).

We can join the fellowship of Christ's sufferings. This enables us to rejoice with those who rejoice and to weep with those who weep. (See Romans 12:15.) The God of compassion and all comfort is always there to help us. (See 2 Corinthians 1:3-4.)

David writes, *"The sacrifices of God are a broken spirit, a broken and contrite heart, O God, you will not despise"* (Ps. 51:17 NIV).

The great evangelist and writer Charles Finney knew and practiced the truth of this verse. He had a weeping heart. He often went into the woods north of his village to pray, and he confessed that he did this so that others would not see him. He writes, "An overwhelming sense of my wickedness in being ashamed to have a human being see me on my knees before God took such a powerful possession of me that I cried at the top of my voice, and I exclaimed that I would not leave, and I proclaimed that I would not leave this place, that if all the men on earth, and all the devils in hell surrounded me. I prayed until my mind became so full that before I was aware of it I was on my feet and tripping up the ascent towards the road."

Though he had gone into the woods at dawn, when he reached town it was already noon. He had been so lost in prayer that time had lost all meaning to him. He later went to dinner but discovered that he had no appetite for food, so he went to his office to play hymns on his bass viola, but he found that he couldn't sing without weeping.

He shares what happened as that night progressed: "All my feelings seemed to rise and to flow out, the utterance of my heart was, I want to pour out my whole soul to God. The rising of my soul was so great, I went…back to the front office to pray, I wept like a child, and made such confession as I could with my choked utterance. It seemed to be as though I bathed His feet with my tears."[5]

This weeping servant sowed precious seed into the lives of two and a half million people who came to know the Lord Jesus Christ as their personal Savior. Research tells us that at least 75 percent of these converts remained true to Christ till their deaths.

This is what we need today—men and women of God who learn the power of tears, the compassion of Christ, the importance of prayer, and the fire of the Holy Ghost.

DO WHAT MATTERS

A few years ago, in one of those times of transition that God loves and we tend to disdain, I was fervently seeking the Lord. Like a shepherd guiding His sheep, Jesus, my Great Shepherd responded to my passionate prayer and gave me a dream of wisdom and guidance. In this enlightening dream in which I was soaring through the heavens like an American Kestrel, a bird that is noted for its ability to hover in the air against even strong winds. Sometimes the kestrel appears to be standing still in mid-air. So, here I was, flying like a bird through the air when suddenly everything stopped. Next, I received a tremendous revelation.

I saw a beautiful garden next to a great stone wall and an attractive stucco-covered house. It was as if I was looking at this scene through a camera's zoom lens. I saw a spectacular array of multicolored flowers and then I saw a woman in a red dress; she was bent over, working in the garden.

Somehow I knew this woman was my Aunt Mae, a wonderful, godly woman, who had inspired my life at a very early age. I remembered the details of her scarlet red dress. She looked up at me and slowly said, "Do...what...matters." That's all I heard in the dream, and then the revelation was over.

This was pictorial representation of my mother's oldest sister, and she was giving me a very important message, as she worked in her garden as she had always loved to do. Aunt Mae gave her life to serve others. She remained single all through her life, and fully presented herself to God, so that He could use her as He desired. This wonderful lady impacted my life in so many important ways in my youth, and still I miss her today, though she has been with the Lord for many years now.

In the dream a voice came to me, "Do what matters." And I knew immediately what the Lord was referring to. What's important in this life? Paul says, "*...The only thing that counts is faith expressing itself through love*" (Gal. 5:6 NIV).

As you get the heart of God, which is love, you can't help but do what matters.

BROUGHT BACK BY THE TEARS OF A FRIEND

When I was in Prague some time ago, I learned that one of the main pastors, Evald Ruffy, of a Moravian church would not be able to be with us because he had suffered a heart attack while ministering in Sweden, and he was in a coma.

His best friend, Peter, called for Christians throughout the Czech Republic to pray for Pastor Ruffy. As he traveled to Sweden to be with the pastor, Peter felt as if he was actually taking the prayers of the saints with him. He said that he could definitely feel the power of their prayers as he walked into the hospital.

An eruption of the Holy Spirit took place within Peter in the entranceway of the hospital, and he was stirred with compassion deep within. Meanwhile, Pastor Evald had already spent three days with God in Heaven, where he discovered many spiritual mysteries.

He was able to look down upon the earth from his heavenly vantage point, and he saw dark clouds all over Central and Eastern Europe. While beholding this scene, he noticed white lights going up and down through the black clouds. He asked his Guide, the Holy Spirit, "What is this?"

"Well, the dark clouds are the territorial spirits of darkness that are over Central Europe."

The pastor raised another question, "What are those white lights?"

"Oh, those are My angels, and they are breaking up the powers of darkness over Central Europe."

"How does this happen?" the pastor asked.

"Oh, this happens in answer to the prayers of the saints."

Pastor Evald was greatly enjoying this special experience that God was giving to him unbeknownst to Peter who was now standing by his friend's bed feeling somewhat helpless. In his weakness, Peter began to cry, weeping profusely over his friend. When his tears streamed down his face and fell onto his friend's face and body, something amazing happened.

Those tears that splashed upon Evald's face caused him to realize that his work on earth was not over. He still had more to do as a husband, father, and pastor. His eyes opened, and he was instantly released from the coma that had imprisoned and immobilized him. In fact, he was totally healed! Even his doctors declared that what happened to him was a miracle.

The power of tears had brought healing to a man of God, a modern-day apostle who went on to establish many Spirit-filled, evangelical Moravian churches in Eastern Europe.

Intercessory prayer combined with compassionate weeping is a powerful force that truly brings change in our world today. As William Booth declared, "Try tears!"

Do you want to move in compassion? Then receive compassion. Do you want to move in healing? Then receive healing. Do you want to move in deliverance? Then receive deliverance. Whatever you receive by faith through the love of God you will be authorized to give away.

Stop by the gateway of the sixth door as I have and drink deeply from the brook of mercy. This will enable you to continue to move forward in your walk of being more like Jesus and empower you to do the works of Christ. Perhaps then, you too, will have a shadow cast from your life like that of Catherine Booth—the Mother of the Salvation Army.

Jesus said, "...*Freely (without pay) you have received, freely (without charge) give"* (Matt. 10:8).

Heavenly Father, your Word declares that you welcome those who have a broken and a contrite heart. Give us your great grace so that we can walk in unison with your heart. Help us to humble ourselves before you, leaning on our beloved Jesus. Lord, grant us the gift of tears and a compassionate heart, so that we would see life spring forth where it seems hopeless and lifeless. We desire your heart, Lord, and we cry, as Ezekiel did so long ago, "Let streams of tears flow into wastelands and bring forth Newness of life, victory, healing, joy, and compassion to those in need. In Jesus' great name. Amen!

ENDNOTES

1. John Wimber, *Power Healing* (San Francisco, CA: Harper, 1987), 47-48.

2. Dick Eastman, *No Easy Road* (Grand Rapids, MI: Baker Books, 1971), 92.

3. Richard Foster, *Prayer: Finding the Heart's True Home* (New York, NY: Harper Collins Publishers, 1992), 39-40.

4. Ibid., 37-38.

5. Dick Eastman, *No Easy Road*, 93.

chapter three

The Mother of the Salvation Army—Catherine Booth

by
Michal Ann Goll

What can we do to wake the Church up? Too often those who have its destinies in the palm of their hands are chiefly chosen from those who are mere encyclopedias of the past rather than from those who are distinguished by their possession of Divine Power. For leadership of the Church something more is required.[1]

Catherine Booth, 1829-1890

A FOOL FOR CHRIST

This chapter focuses on a true heroine of faith and compassion—Catherine Booth. She has paved the way for the liberation and deliverance of women, children, the downtrodden, the forgotten, the lost, and the dying, and from her courageous example we can learn so much.

In Catherine's time very few women ever rose to speak to a church congregation. One day, however, as Catherine was sitting in the Gateshead Bethesda Chapel, she felt a strong urging to rise and speak. As she prepared to do so, she heard an inner voice say, "You will look like a fool and have nothing to say!"

She recognized the voice as being the devil, and she countered with, "That's just the point! I have never yet been willing to be a fool for Christ. Now I will be one!"[2]

I love this lady and the wonderful determination she exhibited in the face of seemingly insurmountable odds. I want to be like her, don't you?

As we begin to study Catherine's life, it is very important to realize how difficult it is to separate her life and accomplishments from her husband, William. William and Catherine exemplify a Barak and Deborah type anointing. Their ministries so blended together and overlapped; the ministry and anointing of one made the other's possible, and visa versa. So, we are going to study both in this chapter. I believe the Lord is releasing in this day the anointing of the Deborah's and the Barak's—serving together, working together, benefiting each other, jealous only for the illumination and presence of God. Now, that's what I'm talking about!

"GOD SHALL HAVE ALL THERE IS OF WILLIAM BOOTH!"

William Booth was born on April 19, 1829, in Nottingham. His father, Samuel, was a builder, but the economic conditions were very poor in England at this time, which meant that the homes he built were not selling. He could neither sell nor rent the homes he built, so he eventually lost everything, including the mortgage on his own house.

Though he had great plans for William, including a good gentleman's education, Samuel did not have enough money to make this happen for his son. Therefore, when William was 13 years old, he was apprenticed to a pawn broker named Francis Eames, who worked in Nottingham's Goose Creek section, a horrible part of the city, where homeless people had to live in the streets.

Less than a year later, Samuel Booth died, so William was faced with the dismal prospects of having to support the family, which included his mother and his sisters. Eventually, his mother was able to find a job running a small shop in Goose Gate, and between their two incomes, they managed to keep food on the family table.[3]

As a result of working in such a poor part of the city, William saw firsthand how the poor had to live and how miserable most of them were. He responded to the misery he saw around him with a sense of gloom and despair until one night in 1844, when he was walking home after work.

Suddenly, a sense of spiritual exaltation flooded his entire being. This was very much like John Wesley's Aldersgate Chapel experience, when the founder of the Methodist Church felt his heart "strangely warmed." In William's case he responded by renouncing his sin and turning his heart and life over to the Lord. This was the earnest declaration he made that night: "God shall have all there is of William Booth!"

Soon thereafter, William began to blend his social consciousness with his newfound faith and a great desire grew within him to see an organization formed that would have the salvation of the world as its supreme ambition and goal. His perspective was a practical one; he wanted to meet the real needs of people. Therefore, he wasn't very much concerned with ecclesiastical creeds, rituals, and forms.

There were a few different preachers, including the American revivalist James Caughey who held evangelistic meetings in Nottingham in 1846, who became William's mentors, and he learned a great deal about God from these men. He also read the sermons and books of John Wesley, George Whitefield, and Charles Finney, particularly Finney's *Lectures on Revivals of Religion.*

William and his friend Will Sansom joined their hearts and hands together by determining to make a difference in the lives of the people of the Meadow Platts neighborhood, a very poor section of the city. Theirs was a roll-up-your-sleeves kind of faith that wasn't afraid to reach out and touch the actual needs of people. It was faith in action, and the compassion these men had in their hearts for the "down and outers" of society was not afraid to *act* in behalf of others.

These two men did more than just hold meetings; they went on to visit and encourage those who made decisions for Christ, and they visited the sick in the community, as well.

This was a time when the average life expectancy, due to disease and other factors, was short—35-40 years of age. Unfortunately, Will Sansom died soon after the two men began their ministry. It was then when William began conducting open-air meetings for the poor in Red Lion's Square and "down in the bottoms," one of Nottingham's cruelest neighborhoods.

Booth wrote, "I saw terrible sights—ragged, shrieking people, little children foraging for food, dirty women, some clad only in soiled petticoats, more little children—these appeared drunk, with their mothers forcing beer down their throats—whimpering, hungry dogs, men's faces with animal passion written all over them as they watched dancing women in the street."[4]

Later, in a letter he sent to Catherine from London, he wrote, "I've been told that there are 3 million souls in London, and 100,000 paupers. After what I've seen this week, I know it's true. Many of these people are on the brink of starvation.... Catherine, the people are sick, some of them dying, some are already dead. And the smell...the whole city stinks, I couldn't escape it.... I've found my destiny. It's a human jungle out there. I've been walking in the midst of it.... It's as bad as any tiger-infested jungle in darkest Africa."

Because of his hard work and his passion for the poor, William Booth became known as "Willful Will." He was very much like the American evangelist Dwight L. Moody who ministered in Chicago later in that same century. Moody said that the world had yet to see what would happen when one man gave his life unreservedly to the Lord, and he said he intended to be that man.

"MY GOD, I AM THINE!"

Now let's take a closer look at the life of Catherine Booth, who was born on January 17, 1829, in Ashburn, Derbyshire. Her maiden name was Mumford. Her father was a rather unstable individual, who exhibited very erratic behavior. At one time he had been a lay preacher in the Methodist Church, then he became a temperance advocate, who preached vigorously against alcohol, but finally he became an alcoholic himself! As you can imagine, he was prone to wild swings of uncontrollable emotions, and all this turmoil and uncertainty must have had a deep impact in the life of Catherine as she was growing up.

As the child of an alcoholic, Catherine knew firsthand what happens to families affected by alcoholism. By the time she was 12, she was able to attend a girls' school and became the secretary of the Juvenile Temperance Society, and had read the Bible all the way through eight times!

When Catherine was 14, she developed a spinal curvature; then, four years later, she came down with incipient tuberculosis, and was home-schooled during much of this time.

Due to her illnesses, she was isolated from other children her age, and this enabled her to cultivate her relationship with her heavenly Father. She read the Bible and also studied church history and theology. Also, this was when her writing career began, as it was while she was sick in bed that she began writing articles for magazines that warned of the dangers of alcohol, and she became a supporter of temperance societies.[5]

When Catherine was 16, she had a radical conversion experience in church on a Sunday morning. This happened because she took to heart the words of a hymn written by Charles Wesley: "My God, I am thine, what a comfort divine, what a blessing to know that Jesus is mine." She surrendered her life to the Lord Jesus Christ, and she knew that He took up His residence in her heart.

Catherine and her mother were attending a Wesleyan Methodist Church at this time, but like so many others, including William, they got caught in the division between the Wesleyan Methodists and the Reformers, which had broken from the Methodist Church because they perceived it to be cold and lifeless, too conservative for their tastes. It was at this point that both William and Catherine were expelled from the Methodist Church.

Their relationship with the Reformers did not last long, however, for the Reformers stressed strong organization and a lot of committee work, which many perceived as detrimental to the more important work of revival.

Catherine's mentors included Charles Finney and John Wesley, and she read many of the same works that her future husband had read.

She became a strong advocate for the unlimited involvement of women in all aspects of worship, teaching, and leadership in the church. Catherine Booth was definitely a woman who was ahead of her time; she was what I call a "breaker" in the Church, one who brings new life and power to the people of God.

"WHAT GOD HAS JOINED TOGETHER..."

In 1852 Catherine met William Booth, a Methodist minister. By this time the Methodist church had lost some of the fervor it had known during the previous century, when the Wesleys—John, Charles, Samuel, and their mother, Susanna—had been instrumental in bringing great change to the church.

William Booth, however, was on fire for God, and he believed that ministers should be involved in "loosing chains of injustice, freeing the captive and oppressed, sharing food and home, clothing the naked, and carrying out family responsibilities." He was a man who was committed to compassionate reform.[6]

Though they loved each other deeply, William and Catherine did have their differences. One of these involved the role of women in the church. These were days in which women were not permitted to minister in the church. Even William Booth regarded them as "the weaker sex," and this aggravated Catherine very much. She could not believe how prejudiced her husband was with regard to women, and she said, "Oh, prejudice, what will it not do, that woman is in any respect, except physical strength and courage, inferior to man, I cannot see cause to believe, and I am sure no one can prove it from the Word of God."

Initially William was strongly opposed to the idea of women preachers, and he based this position on what Paul had written, *"The women should keep quiet in the churches, for they are not authorized to speak, but should take a secondary and subordinate place, just as the Law also says"* (1 Cor. 14:34). I believe that this Scripture has been misinterpreted for centuries, not taking into account that Paul was referring to women who had previously been temple prostitutes, newly converted to Christianity, and untaught in appropriate behavior and customs within the Christian context.

However, Catherine believed that God loved women as much as He loved men and that He had endowed women with qualities and gifts that were equal to those He gave to men.

As time went on, William began to rethink his position on this issue, and he said, "I would not encourage a woman to begin preaching, although I would not stop her on any account."

His focus was on the salvation of the world, so he said, "I am for the world's salvation; I will quarrel with no means that promises help." Here we see his attitude concerning the role of women beginning to undergo some change.

This couple, despite their differences, was sold out to God. Catherine once wrote these words to her husband: "The nearer our assimilation to Jesus, the more perfect and heavenly our union." They knew that for their marriage to work they had to put God first.

William was now beginning to learn things about his wife that he had not known before. He discovered that in conversation she was someone who could hold her own with anyone. She was a very intelligent lady who was conversant with many different things.

For example, she was able to discuss current trends in the churches of England, and she was very much concerned about the controversy swirling between the Revivalists and the anti-revival movement. In addition, Catherine understood the plight of the poor.

Sometimes William would fall victim to fits of gloom and depression. At such times Catherine would stir him up again and give him fresh reasons for battling on. He began to recognize her as his equal and to see that her capacity for work and self-sacrifice was as strong as his. She was both a stimulant and a stabilizer for her husband.

Catherine's compelling and heart-touching writings became well-known throughout England, and she became known simply as "the woman preacher."

In the early days of her public ministry she spoke these strong words about her role: "I dare say many of you have been looking on me as a very devoted woman, but I have been disobeying God. I am convinced that women have the right and duty to speak up; yes, even to preach! I have struggled with this for a long time, but I'll struggle with it no longer."

When William heard his wife preach, he completely changed his mind about women preachers! He did so in spite of the fact that many people judged him for doing so and continued to feel that women preachers were unbiblical.[7]

Lord Shaftesbury, a well-known politician and evangelist, actually declared that William Booth was the antichrist due to his attitude toward women preachers! This did not seem to faze William, however, for he commented, "The best men in my army are the women."[8]

Catherine went on to teach Bible studies, visit in the homes of the poor, and reach out to women, who were greatly abused and oppressed. She made this observation, "The plight of the women is so pathetic."[9]

Here we see the birth of a woman preacher, who became a heroine and mentor to thousands of women, but she was never ordained. Nonetheless, during the first few months of 1861, while the Civil War was raging in the America, Catherine began accepting invitations to preach in public.

She and William served in several different communities, including Gateshead, a town of 50,000, which is located just across the River Tyne from Newcastle on the northeastern coast of England.

When William became sick during the summer of 1860, Catherine had to take over all his duties, for it took him several months to recover. As a result, her remarkable abilities became known to many and her fame as "the woman preacher" grew far and wide.

TRAILBLAZER FOR WOMEN

Nineteenth-century England was a place of many problems. As a result of the Industrial Revolution, poverty, crime, disease, corruption, prostitution, alcoholism, and immorality were rampant. We read about some of these conditions in the novels of social realism that were written by Charles Dickens during this same era.

The Beer Bill of 1830 allowed pubs to be legally open from 4 A.M. to 10 P.M., and many people would spend their meager wages on beer and ale. Decades of beer drinking brought forth an entire generation of drunkards who lost sight of all moral values. Mothers would even serve beer to their small children, who became alcoholics before they reached puberty.

Working conditions were horrendous for everyone, especially women and children. While working with the poor in London, Catherine Booth learned about "sweated labor," women and children who had to work for long hours for very low wages in the worst imaginable conditions.[10]

In certain London tenements Catherine found seamstresses, for example, who had to hem and stitch for 11 hours or more each day! Their pay in comparison to the wages received by men was abysmally low.[11]

Catherine's work among the poor grew into a ministry that seemed as powerful as her husband's preaching, and she continued to preach the Gospel in spite of the multiple criticisms she and her husband received.

When she became aware of a pamphlet that was written by a Rev. A.A. Reese, which was a diatribe against the ministry of Phoebe Palmer, who ministered in both England and America and wrote *The Way of Holiness and Faith and Its Effects,* Catherine responded by writing a booklet of her own entitled, *Female Teaching: or the Reverend A.A. Reese vs. Mrs. Palmer, Being a Reply to a Pamphlet by the Above Named Gentleman on the Sunderland Revival* in which she voiced her support of Phoebe's ministry.

There can be no doubt about it, Catherine Booth was a true trailblazer for women and she was a model of Christian compassion at work in the world.

THE FRUIT OF THEIR LABORS

The Booths' first evangelistic work began on August 11, 1861, in Cornwall County. Originally planned as a seven-week revival, the crusade was extended to an 18-month campaign, which was unparalleled in that part of England, at least since the time of John Wesley.

At least 7,000 Cornishmen found peace with God during this year and a half. It was even reported that fishermen sailed ten miles across dark and choppy waters to hear the young couple preach. Similarly, it was not unusual for villagers to walk several miles to attend the meetings. As a result, many shop owners experienced a great decline in sales, because people's hearts were turning away from material things to God above.

There was a great hunger for God in the hearts of the people. This included Catherine's father, who returned to the Lord. The Booths' outreach was not limited to church people; and they discovered that people who frequented the pubs were more likely to go through a tent flap than through an oaken church door to find God.

William Booth recognized the fact that the clergy weren't reaching the people who had the greatest needs, and he wondered how he would be able to unite his ministry with that of the local church. He wanted his converts to be able to find a "church home."

Therefore, the Booths began to look for ways to connect evangelism to the local church.

He said, "We must find it, we must find it, there's got to be a way."

Many of the new converts, when they went to churches, were greatly disappointed by the stale traditionalism they found there.

BRINGING THE POOR
AND THE WEALTHY TOGETHER

Another cry in the hearts of William and Catherine Booth was to find a way to bring the poor and wealthy together. Therefore, William boldly took the poor into the wealthiest churches of Nottingham. His approach was not well-received by the established church. All this friction stirred them to action, and they left the Reformers and joined a group called the Methodist New Connection, which had a strong Wesleyan foundation, supported revivalism, and encouraged lay people to get involved in the decision making.

This organization had a magazine, and this gave Catherine a great opportunity to continue her writing ministry.

In the spring of 1857, at the annual conference of the Methodist New Connection, William was removed from his position as a full-time evangelist, because some of the leaders of the organization were no longer comfortable with his methods. Therefore, they wanted him to take a regular preaching circuit, which would force him to focus on pastoral responsibilities rather than evangelism.

The particular circuit to which William was assigned was obscure and unsuccessful. The leaders must have felt that this was the perfect place to "keep him out of trouble." William endured this assignment, but did not really like it, and in the meantime Catherine's ministry continued to flourish.

The following year William was ordained as a minister of the Gospel of Jesus Christ, and his next pastoral assignment was in Gateshead. This is when real release began to happen in the Booths' ministry, and their evangelistic outreach began to surge. At this point the young couple began to experiment with publicity, and they distributed handbills door to door throughout every neighborhood. They also conducted street meetings, which consisted of hymn singing, exhortations, and invitations to attend church services.

In an effort to meet the needs of people where they were, the Booths began to take the popular melodies and tunes of their day and adapt them for use as Gospel songs. They made their ministry relevant to the needs of the people.

Before their meetings would begin, the Booths would set aside an entire day of prayer, and this had a great impact on the services, paving the way for the Spirit of God to find entrance into the prepared hearts and lives of the people who attended.

William and Catherine loved the people, and the people responded to their love, which reflected the Father's heart to them.

THE SALVATION ARMY IS BORN

On August 7, 1878, William declared his vision for the Salvation Army. He said, "To postpone action any further will be an act of disobedience to what we both sense is the divine will of God."

Catherine was in full support of this declaration. She said, "William, don't hold back because of me. I can trust in God and go out with Him, and I can live on bread and water. Go out and do your duty. God will provide if we will only go straight on in the path of duty."

It was at this point that they broke with the Methodist New Connection and began their own independent evangelistic ministry. The distinguishing features of this ministry were authority, obedience, the adapted employment of everyone's abilities, the training and discipline of all workers, and the combined action of all.

They adapted army jargon in their work. William believed very much in the chain of command, and he became a general, whose job was to oversee the ministry. They trained the people who worked with them and taught them how to endure and rise above the mocking of the crowds which sometimes occurred.

The idea of uniforms began to emerge at this point, as well, and the bonnets for the women were designed in such a way as to protect them from rotten eggs and garbage that were sometimes thrown at them.

The Booths expected their workers to go into the most distressful situations and love the most needy, most hurting, and sometimes even the most hateful! They also believed in the importance of combining their forces like a mighty army as they reached out to those in need.

At this stage in their lives William and Catherine Booth were only 32 years old. They had five children and very little money. They settled in Leeds, a town in the English midlands, and began to conduct separate campaigns so as to increase their effectiveness.

Hundreds of adults and children responded to the invitation to find Christ under Catherine's preaching ministry in south and west London. Her preaching, along with the success William was experiencing in his ministry to the poor, came to the notice of *The Revival*, England's premier evangelistic journal.

As a result, William was invited to preach in White Chapel in early 1865. White Chapel was a poor section in the notorious East End of London. He asked Catherine to preach there, as well.

Soon thereafter, Catherine became aware of the Midnight Movement for Fallen Women, an agency that combined evangelism with social redemption. Her experience with this organization opened her eyes to the need for social concern to become a part of their ministry.

Catherine began to see a need to champion the cause of women, and she advocated for them to be placed in positions of responsibility and usefulness within the church. Through her preaching in the West End she touched the hearts and lives of people who could help provide financial support for the struggling work William was doing in the East End.

When speaking publicly, Catherine never minced her words. She spoke with boldness and righteous indignation as she confronted the evils of her day. In so doing she made the comfortable less comfortable, and she even went so far as to accuse affluent Christians by saying that they were responsible for the sweatshops and the filthy working conditions in which women and children found themselves.

Once she made this statement, "It will be a happy day for England when Christian ladies transfer their sympathies from poodles and terriers to destitute and starving children."

The Booths then created the East London Christian Revival Society, which became known as the East London Christian Mission, or more commonly, the Christian Mission. This later became known as the Salvation Army. Catherine became the primary promoter of this ministry, while William continued to work among the poor in the East End.

What a team they were! Catherine was doing the preaching and raising the funds, and William was in the trenches, ministering to the needs of the poor.

Early on their children learned what ministry was all about. Their oldest child, William Bramwell Booth, was dedicated to God when he was born. Catherine said, "I held him up to God as soon as I had strength to do so, and I remember specially desiring that he should be an advocate of holiness."

Ballington, their second son, began to see himself as a preacher when he was 11. He even preached to his sisters' dolls! One of his "new converts" was a pillow in a chair. Looking at this pillow, he commanded, "Give up the drink, brother!"

The younger children were Kate, Herbert, Emma, and Marion, who was an invalid, and then along came Evaline Corey, who eventually became the first woman general of the Salvation Army, and Lucy. They had a total of eight children, and each became active in the work of the Salvation Army.

Their children said that Catherine not only patched their clothing, but she even made them proud of the patches!

Bramwell recalled that his father once took him into a pub in the East End of London where he saw the men's alcohol-inflamed faces and observed drunken, disheveled women nursing their babies! He caught the pungent aroma of gin, tobacco, and sweat, and he was nauseated. His father turned to him and said, "These are our people; these are the people I want you to live for and bring to Christ."

Catherine Booth organized Food-for-the-Millions shops, where the poor could afford inexpensively priced hot soup and three-course dinners. On special occasions, such as Christmas, she would sometimes cook more than 300 dinners that were distributed to the poor.

By 1882 there were almost 17,000 people worshiping under the auspices of the Salvation Army, far more than the attendance in mainline churches. This caused the Archbishop of York, the Rev. Dr. William Thornton, to comment that the Salvation Army was reaching people that the Church of England had failed to reach.

Since those early days and more than a century later, the Salvation Army remains a vital force in the world. As a result of the army's ministry, new laws protecting women and children were enacted in England. The impact of the Salvation Army was reached around the world and its ministries have included prison work, youth work, rescue homes for women, ministry to alcoholics and drug addicts, rescue missions, salvage operations, disaster relief, and men's hostels.

The Salvation Army has earned the respect of the White House, the United States Supreme Court, embassies around the world, the U.S. Congress, and governments in many nations.

Catherine Booth was the mother of the Salvation Army—a true "mother in Israel."

Catherine knew that compassion acts; and she also knew that it is born out of passion for the Father's heart. She wrote, "Don't let controversy hurt your soul. Live near to God by prayer. Just fall down at his feet and open your very soul before him, and throw yourself right into his arms."

Father God, thank you for the wonderful example of Catherine Booth. Help us to be like her, people of compassion, who fall at your feet and open our souls before you. We throw ourselves into your arms, dear Father, and ask you to light the fires of passion in our hearts, that we would be aflame with your love and go forth in compassion to those who need to know how much you love them. Let us become true agents of change in the world, as we act in mercy to others. May their lives be completely transformed by your grace and may they see that you truly are their Father. Give us your wisdom, Lord, so we can see things from your point of view. Help us not to lean upon our own insight, but to trust you for all things. As we acknowledge you, we know you will direct our paths. Thank you, Father. In Jesus' name, Amen.

ENDNOTES

1. Catherine Booth, *Women's Wisdom Through the Ages* (New York, NY: Testament Books, 1994), 67.

2. "Catherine Booth." http://www.Spartacus.schoolnet.co.uk/Wbooth.htm.

3. Ibid.

4. Ibid.

5. Ibid.

6. Ibid.

7. Ibid.

8. Ibid.

9. Helen K. Hosier, *William and Catherine Booth: Founders of The Salvation Army: Heroes Of The Faith* (Uhrichsville, OH: Barbour Publishing, 1999), 58.

10. Ibid., 76-77.

11. http://www.Spartacus.schoolnet.co.uk/Wbooth.htm.

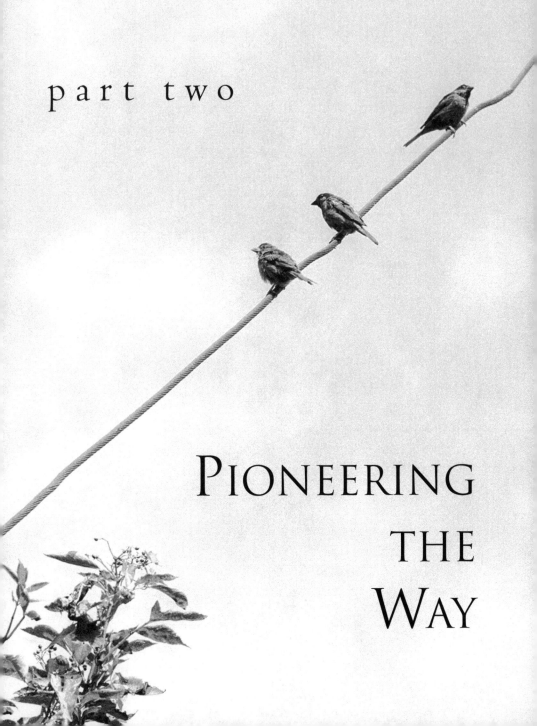

part two

PIONEERING
THE
WAY

P art two is devoted to nine women who spent their lives in compassionate service to God and others:

Nancy Ward, who became known as "the last beloved lady" of the Cherokee Nation, because of her heroism, her advocacy in behalf of women, and her compassionate service to others.

Florence Nightingale, who was instrumental in the reform of health care and the establishment of a well-trained nursing profession. She personally ministered to thousands of wounded soldiers during the Crimean War.

Gladys Aylward, who was a small woman of great faith and a missionary to China during the 20th century. You will be stirred by the accounts of her service to the sick, the orphans, and the poor in China.

Mother Teresa, who is considered by many to be the most compassionate woman of the 20th century because of her work among the poor in Calcutta, India. Because of her devotion to God and the people she served, this diminutive woman has become a giant in the Kingdom of God.

Amy Carmichael, who was a missionary in India for more than 50 years. She served God faithfully throughout her life and brought His compassion to Indian girls who had been offered as temple prostitutes by their parents. She became a great writer, as well.

Catherine Drexel, who was known as "the millionaire nun," because she gave away millions of dollars to those in need, particularly to help impoverished Native American Indians and African Americans.

Phoebe Palmer, who was a great influence in the spread of the Holiness Movement throughout the United States and around the world. This handmaiden of the Lord knew that true compassion stems from holiness and righteousness before God.

Hannah More, who, as a well-known writer, became a trailblazer for women everywhere. She also worked diligently for the abolition of slavery along with her friends William Wilber-force and John Newton.

Elizabeth Fry, who was a Quaker and a prison reformer in England and Europe. Her work did much to alleviate the unjust suffering and torture of prisoners, the sick, and the mentally ill.

These nine women and many others have pioneered the way so that God's compassion might be expressed in new and creative ways in the lives of countless millions of people around the world. It is our prayer that your heart will be stirred as you read these stories. But we also desire that these stories will become sources of inspiration so that you will become a pioneer of compassion in your own world.

chapter four

Beloved Woman of the Cherokee—Nancy Ward

Nan-ye-hi (Nancy Ward), Ghighau (Beloved Woman)
of the Ani-Yunwiya (Principal People)

by
Ada Winn with Dr. J. Mark Rodgers

A fresh wind is blowing within the Body of Christ. Across denominational, racial, and political lines the Spirit of God is exposing the roots of ritual-based, Christian religion. This exposure is showing many of us ways in which our religious expressions have supplanted an authentic relationship with the fullness of the Father. Starting down this path of the revelation of our citizenship in God's Kingdom we begin to encounter many paradigms. Paradigms for whatever reason, we may have chosen to ignore. Comfort in America is being displaced with a kind of holy unrest. It is in this place of holy unrest that we begin to collide with realities which are uncomfortable to look directly in the eye.

Whether or not we like to admit it, the cultures that most dramatically shaped our nation as we know it were those of the Greeks and Romans. Even in this modern era, their societies continue to influence government structures, health care delivery systems, educational institutions and perhaps most importantly, religious structures in America. It is the third century Roman church that is responsible for when we worship, where we worship, how we worship and with whom we worship. It is said that Christian faith conquered Rome and then Rome conquered Christianity. It is out of a conquering mind-set that most people view American history. Perhaps one of God's Kingdom perspectives is viewing America from a lens other than that of July 4, 1776. Could it be that God views the United States from a minority status as well as seeing the vast accomplishments that we now enjoy?

Over the millennia, European societies developed along the lines of artificially supported living environments. I use the phrase "artificially supported living environments" to describe a community that has to go outside the bounds of its territory for the basics of health and welfare. These societies exploited environmental conditions for the purpose of gaining greater wealth and opulence. Wealth represented power and power, in turn, controls.

During this same time period, Native American societies lived in cooperation with their environment. This contrasts the ideals of exploitation versus stewardship. When Europeans arrived on the North American continent, they found a pristine environment with little impact from thousands of years of human habitation. European societies had a need for industrial revolution where Native Americans did not. Native America would never have found need for such endeavors since their society was empowered by the land in which they dwelled. Having been left to their own devices, Native American culture more than likely would have continued on its path of environmental harmony. First-nation people did not have philosophies or religious basics toward a concept of taking more from the land than they needed. Wealth and status achieved thru exploitation of the land was contrary to the fabric of their society. It is out of thousands of years of stewardship that we examine the life of one Native American we know as Nancy Ward.[1]

Her native name was Nan-ye-hi. As was the custom of many Europeans, we simply refused to learn the language and anglicized her name into Nancy. Out of respect for her, I will use her native name for the remainder of this chapter. She was born sometime around 1737 in Chota, the capital of the Cherokee nation. Nan-ye-hi was described as a strikingly beautiful woman with a tall erect figure, prominent nose, piercing black eyes, and silken black hair. Because her skin was tinted like a reddish-pink rose, she was given the nickname *Tsistuna-gis-ka,* or "Wild Rose." As she grew older, Nan-ye-hi matured with a stately but kind disposition, carrying herself with a queenly and majestic character.

Cherokee societies were matrilineal. Warriors received their status in the tribe, not from their father's lineage, but from their mother's. It was in this matrilineal society that women derived their basics of life in the tribe. Women were stewards of the land, not the men. The women enjoyed more matrimonial rights than men. Upon marriage, the men became members of their wife's clan. Their homes along with its contents belonged to the women. Children belonged to the mother's clan. It was into matrilineal lines of the tribal leadership that Nan-ye-hi was born.

Her mother was said to have been Tame Doe. Tame Doe was a niece of Old Hop. Old Hop was a principle chief. One of Tame Doe's brothers was Attakullakulla, a celebrated Peace Chief. Historians rated him as one of the most influential Indian leaders among Southern Tribes. He was named "Little Carpenter" by the whites because of his diplomatic skills. These skills included fitting parts of peace treaties together into a workable diplomatic document.

Nan-ye-hi married early by today's standards. She married King Fisher while only 16 years of age. King Fisher was a leader within the tribe. His leadership was tested during one of the fiercest battles recorded in Cherokee history, the battle of Taliwa. Led by their great war chief, Oconostota, the Cherokee were determined to drive the Muskogean, or Creeks, out of their land. In 1755, Creek opponents reportedly outnumbered a 500-man Cherokee war party. In support of her husband, Nan-ye-hi was "chewing" the musket balls for his rifle. This chewing of the soft musket balls was done in hopes that they would become more lethal. I imagine King Fisher was both directing his men in battle as well as watching over his young bride.

There were war whoops and screams, the sound of musket fire and the yelling of commands over the din of the battle. King Fisher was struck down in the midst of the fight. His mortal wound, more than likely, occurred while attempting to gain a better advantage to lead his tribe to victory. It is said this injury occurred at the lowest ebb of fighting.

I imagine that husband and wife glanced at each other for one brief moment realizing the tragedy that had befallen them. This 16-year-old bride witnessed the flicker of life leave her mortally wounded husband, an event not uncommon for many Cherokee women on the day of that battle. I am sure King Fisher's closest warriors came to his side, consoling the heart of a widowed child in the midst of what looked like defeat. It was at this time when Nan-ye-hi distinguished herself from other women. Even though it was common for a woman to support her warrior husband, it was very uncharacteristic for this young girl to join in the battle and continue the fight. Her unwavering bravery that day rallied the Cherokee warriors and routed the Muskogee's from northern Georgia.

After the appropriate time of mourning, the tribe celebrated Nan-ye-hi's efforts in this nationally significant battle by bestowing upon her the honor of Ghighau or "Beloved Woman." Nan-ye-hi was in her teens when vaulted into her high position—an honor ordinarily bestowed on older women. Ghighau was more than a term of endearment; it enabled Nan-ye-hi to participate in negotiations for treaties, to commute death sentences passed upon by tribal leadership, and to prepare portions of ceremonial offerings given to the men of the tribe. The Beloved Woman title was a lifetime distinction. During state counsel meetings in the townhouse, Ghighau sat with the Peace Chief and War Chief in the Holy Area near the ceremonial fire. As head of the Women's Counsel, she would represent the view of women in the tribe. The female counsel did not hesitate to vote to oppose the decisions made by the ruling headsmen, particularly if they felt that the welfare of the tribe was at stake. It was during the lifetime of Nan-ye-hi that tribal leadership passed all but two of the land cession treaties with the Cherokee.

During the 1700s, European settlers began in earnest to encroach upon Cherokee lands. Discovery of the New World triggered a long struggle for control and supremacy between European nations. The surge of newly arriving immigrants increased annually. These newcomers pressed westward, as settlements grew crowded in the east. They saw vast stretches of wilderness seemingly uninhabited except for scattered tribal villages. All native people were viewed as inhabitants having no recorded claim or title to the land. Because there was little civil government along the frontier, Europeans moved into Indian territories one way or another. Settlers from the east were simply not going to be contained by the physical barrier of the Appalachian Mountains. The British government was growing more and more incapable of ruling the colonies and King George III had forbidden development of lands west of the Appalachian Mountains. As rising unrest was apparent as the colonies prepared for war against British rule, the land to the west was simply too enticing.

Spaniards viewed all native people of the America's as a curiosity. This curiosity posed no serious threat to their interests. Colonists saw them as ignorant savages. They continued to view native society from the viewpoint of Roman dominated thinking. Natives were to be exploited and pushed out of the way. To the white man, land was an object of trade or barter. The vast wilderness offered farming space. The forests were filled with wild game. This game offered meat for the table and pelts that could be sold or traded. All of this land along with its many resources appeared free for the taking.

Trade between the native people and Europeans was more exploitation than market place equality. Oftentimes trade goods were of inferior nature, with firearms misfiring and leaving Indians injured. The demand of animal skins to pay their debts to the English traders increased yearly. Hunting was changed from an enjoyable act of providing for their family to an ever-increasing business proposition. Up until 1750, an average of 54,000 deerskins per year were shipped from Charles Town (today known as Charleston, South Carolina). By 1759, it is said that over 1.5 million deerskins were shipped annually through the Charles Town port. This "big kill," as it is called, almost exhausted the deer population in the South.

Native American immune systems were not accustomed to many European diseases. From the outset of European contact, small pox, scarlet fever, and measles killed by the millions. In some cases American colonists used these diseases as a form of biologic terror. One American general wrote of his introduction of disease-contaminated blankets into native populations in the hopes "it would have the desired result." More died in this American holocaust than died in Hitler's concentration camps during World War II.

The fledgling independence movement found its way across the Appalachian Mountains into what is now eastern Tennessee. Having to face either the tyranny of British rule or hostile Indians, some chose to face the Cherokee. Despite stern warnings from the Crown of England for all white settlers to leave native land west of the Appalachian Mountains, settlements at Watauga and Nolichucky were created.

The Cherokees' first reaction was not war. The Cherokee tribal council negotiated a ten-year lease agreement with the Wataugans. In exchange for this land lease, they were to receive the equivalent of a $1,000 per year in trade goods. Their desire was to live peacefully alongside the white settlers while they remained stewards of the land. The Wataugans also agreed to no further encroachment on native lands. There was a peaceful coexistence during the early years of the lease. This peace was short lived when the settlers continued to want more land while not providing trade goods as promised.

After many violated treaties by the settlers, a battle erupted during the summer of 1776 with the Wataugan and Nolichucky settlements. Nan-ye-hi sent messages to Fort Watauga and the surrounding communities warning of an attack. Some might question her motives in warning the settlers; however her desire was to live peacefully with the white population. The Cherokee, led by Dragging Canoe, Nan-ye-hi's cousin, were defeated by the settlers due to the preparation before the attack. The attack on Fort Watauga was repelled.

During this battle, Chief Old Abram captured two prisoners who were taken back to Cherokee villages. One of the captives was a Mrs. William Bean. She was tied to a pole with leather thongs and dry tree branches were laid around her feet and lit on fire. When Nan-ye-hi learned of the planned execution, she kicked the burning branches away, stomped out the remaining small flames, and cut the throngs, diffidently freeing Mrs. Bean. She then addressed the angered warriors and spoke with harsh words, "It revolts my soul that Cherokee warriors would stoop so low as to torture this woman. No woman shall be tortured or burned at the stake while I am Honored Woman."

This incident shows Nan-ye-hi exercising her official position as Ghighau. Nan-ye-hi led Mrs. Bean to her home in Chota, the town of sanctuary. She asked Mrs. Bean to teach her and the members of her family how to process cow's milk to make butter and cheese. She was hoping to encourage interest in her people for raising their own meat and farm crops. Dependence solely on dwindling wildlife, resources of the forest and expensive supplies would spell certain failure of her people. Nan-ye-hi also learned the art of weaving cloth, or home spun, by Mrs. Bean. When it was safe to do so, Nan-ye-hi sent Mrs. Bean back to her home. Nan-ye-hi's son, Five Killer, and her brother, Long Fellow, escorted Mrs. Bean to protect her during the journey.

It was sometime during this timeframe when Nan-ye-hi met a trader named Bryant Ward. Some believe that Nan-ye-hi and her friends protected the life of this trader during a time of hostility. Bryant Ward and Nan-ye-hi were married shortly there after. As a woman in a matrilineal society, she had rights to take a husband as she pleased, even when this choice is outside of her race. What is more interesting is that she took his last name in direct conflict with her cultural upbringing. You may recall that the men took their wife's heritage after marriage. Nan-ye-hi was sending yet another message that it was possible to make changes in order to preserve a way of life.

Throughout Nan-ye-hi's life, her tribe was approached many times about additional acquisitions of land. More than 500 treaties would be signed with the native peoples of America; only two were ever kept by either the British or American government. Hostilities continued to flare as native warriors retaliated for white encroachments; and white settlers exacted their revenge on native populations for what they felt were atrocities. Nan-ye-hi found herself continuously in a place of attempting to mediate between warring factions.

Another flare-up occurred between the Over Mountain Men of the Watauga settlement shortly after the battle of Kings Mountain. The British had promised that they would invade the southern coastland and join forces with the Cherokee to drive the independent white settlers off of Indian land. This had great appeal to Dragging Canoe and tribal leadership; however, the British were unable to make good their threat. This prevented the Cherokee and the British from a frontal and rear attack at the colonies. It became quite apparent to the Cherokee that if they were going to war against the whites, they needed to immediately take action on their own. Nan-ye-hi again found herself forewarning frontier settlers of an eminent attack by Dragging Canoe. She saw that every time the Cherokee were on the warpath, her nation suffered tragically. She had witnessed indiscriminant killing on both sides. Perhaps she hoped that by sending her warning much bloodshed could be avoided. Keep in mind that Nan-ye-hi never acted alone in any of these warnings to frontier settlers. Her tribal leadership had met and voted to continue peacefully. The warring chiefs would not listen to those who were in leadership of the tribe. In sending warning of attack, Nan-ye-hi was representing what she thought was the true nature of official tribal leadership.

A new treaty was demanded by the Cherokee in order to prevent future battles with the new American colonies. Nan-ye-hi rose from the negotiations and eloquently addressed both parties present. "You know that women are always looked upon as nothing, but we are your mothers. You are our sons. Our cry is all for peace. Let it continue. This peace must last forever. Let your women's sons be ours, our sons be yours, let your women hear our words." The sincerity and appeal of her words reached the hearts of her listeners.

Colonel William Christian was chosen to answer Nan-ye-hi's comments. "Mothers, we have listened well to your talk. It is humane. No man can hear it without being moved by it. Such words and thoughts show the world that human nature is the same everywhere. Our women shall hear your words and we know how they will feel and think of them. We are all descendants of the same woman. We will not quarrel with you because you are our mothers. We will not meddle with your people if they will be still and quite at home and let us live in peace." This is one of the very few treaties, if not the only one, that did not ask for land.

Her talk placed Nan-ye-hi in the ranks of great women of America. The time of her talk was July 1781. Nan-ye-hi had witnessed the burning and pillage of her tribe. She had every right to be bitter in seeing everything she loved destroyed; however, she chose a different path—the path of peace. It took fortitude and character for any woman warrior not to strike back.

By 1784, Nan-ye-hi Ward's home in the beloved town of Chota would no longer remain a prominent place in Cherokee history. It was burned and pillaged first by the British and later by American colonists. Legend has it that prior to Nan-ye-hi moving from Chota, she opened her home to orphaned Indian children (mostly outcasts, abandoned, half-breed children, waifs of white traders and Indian women)—perhaps, the only real sanctuary these youngsters enjoyed. A Lieutenant Francis Marion wrote with eloquent terms what he saw take place.

"We proceeded by Colonel Grant's orders to burn the Indian cabins.... I saw everywhere around the footsteps of little Indian children where they had lately played under the shade of their rustling corn. When we are gone, thought I, they will return and peeping through the weeds with tearful eyes will mark the ghastly ruin where they had so often played. 'Who did this?' they will ask their mothers and the reply will be, 'The white people did it, the Christians did it.' Thus for cursed mammon's sake, the followers of Christ have sowed the selfish tares of hate...."

Nan-ye-hi continued as an advocate for her country and nation for several years. She continued to speak of the necessity of her people to devote more attention to farming and raising stock as a means of survival. Nan-ye-hi's seeds were sown in fertile soil and one of the last treaties with the Cherokee, Article 14 of the Holston River Treaty, guaranteed their ability and assistance in husbandry and agriculture as they continued to prosper in their land.

Another attempt at peace occurred in a meeting at Hopewell, North Carolina. This meeting was the first meeting of the United States Congress with any Indian nation. Congress disavowed all previous treaties promising the rights of the Cherokee to live on their land. Concessions were made to return parts of their territory then under control of white settlers. This agreement became known as the Hopewell treaty. The Hopewell treaty granted the Cherokee the right to remove any white settler from their homeland by force if necessary. The United States Congress never kept this agreement. Furthermore, they did not support the Cherokee when they began to remove settlers from their lands.

After the Hopewell Treaty failed miserably, other treaties were forthcoming. The treaties of 1817-1819 further eroded Cherokee homelands. United States commissioners resorted to bribery and other illegal means to obtain signers. The 2,000 who had already moved west were told they could have no western land until an equivalent acreage had been ceded in the east. This of course was a lie. As a result of this falsehood, 15 western Cherokee chiefs were persuaded to sign by proxy. Well-placed bribes enticed 31 eastern chiefs to sign. The eastern chiefs who signed the cession papers moved west, fearful for their lives. By this time official Cherokee council leadership had passed a law that any chief that ceded additional land would be put to death. The transaction was bitterly resented by the Cherokee council and rejected by Cherokee national mandate.

Nan-ye-hi Ward addressed her nation for the last time on May 2, 1817:

"The Cherokee ladies now being present at the meetings of the chiefs and warriors in counsel have thought it their duty as mothers to address their beloved chiefs and warriors now assembled.

"Our beloved children and head men of the Cherokee nation we address you warriors in counsel we have raised all of you on the land which we now have, which God gave us to inhabit and raise provisions we know that our country has once been extensive but by repeated sales has become circumscribed to a small tract and never have thought it our duty to interfere in the disposition of it until now, if a father or mother was to sell all their lands which they had to demand on which their children had to raise their living on which would be indeed bad and to be removed to another country we do not wish to go to any unknown country which we have understood some of our children wish to go over the Mississippi but this act of our children would be like destroying your mothers. Your mothers, your sisters ask and beg of you not to part with any more of our lands, we say ours you are descendants and take pity on our request, but keep it for our growing children for it was the good will of our creator to place us here and you know our father, the great president will not allow his white children to take our country away only keep your hands off of paper talks for it is our own country for if it was not they would not ask you to put your hands to paper for it would be impossible to remove us all for as soon as one child is raised we have others in our arms for such is our situation and will consider our circumstance.

"Therefore children don't part with any more of our lands but continue on it and enlarge your farms and cultivate and raise corn and cotton and we your mothers and sisters will make clothing for you which our father, the president, has recommended to us all we don't charge anybody for selling any lands, but we have heard such intentions of our children but your talks become true at last and it was our desire to forewarn you all not to part with our lands.

"Nancy Ward to her children Warriors to take pity and listen to talks of your sisters, although I am very old yet cannot but pity the situation in which you will hear of their minds, I have great many grandchildren, which I wish them to do well on our land."

This address was taken to the counsel meeting by Nan-ye-hi's son, Five Killer, and accompanied by her distinctive walking cane, which represented her official vote and authority in her absence.

Nan-ye-hi made one final attempt to stay on her land prior to her death. One stipulation of the 1817-1819 treaty had a reservation clause: "Each head of a Cherokee family residing on lands herein or hereafter ceded to the United States who elects to become a citizen of the United States shall receive a reservation of six hundred and forty (640) acres to include his or her improvements for life, with reversion in fee simple to children, subject to widow's dower." Nan-ye-hi's Reservation number 767 was registered with United States government. The State of Tennessee flatly refused to recognize these individual reservation grants.

Nan-ye-hi died in the Amovey district near the Ocoee River at the home of her brother, Long Fellow. Her white husband left her for other relationships; however they continued to be friends. Ward's white family reportedly received her with great respect when they visited on occasion. She lived a long and fruitful life. She has been called Princess and Prophetess. Some referred to her as that beautiful, winsome and resourceful woman, Nancy Ward.

Nan-ye-hi, and those she represented, planted many seeds in her nation that would not come of age until after her death. By the time of the Indian Removal Act of 1838, the Cherokee nation had a form of government similar to that of the colonies. They had a supreme court; the tribe elected their leadership; they had a newspaper and a written language and had adapted many of the ways of the colonists. It was against the Cherokee constitution for anyone to hold official office within the nation that did not have a belief in God. The unofficial Cherokee national anthem became "Amazing Grace."

I had the privilege of visiting Nan-ye-hi's home site near Benton, Tennessee. Her gravesite is now a Tennessee Historic Site. I have visited many hallowed places from Plymouth Rock to the Freedom Hall in Philadelphia, Pennsylvania. There is a stillness in such places—an honor—that feels very tangible.

This chapter regarding the life of Nan-ye-hi is not simply a historic visitation for me as an individual. My family was in Fort Watauga during the time period of Dragging Canoe's attacks. It is highly likely that Nan-ye-hi's two warnings to these settlements may well have saved my family's life—ultimately, saving my own. Could it be that neither my children nor I would enjoy this life without her compassion for the early settlers of Tennessee?

As I walked her land my heart was grateful for the compassionate acts of this wonderful lady I have never met. It would be interesting to know who else walks this country today who does not know they are alive because of Nan-ye-hi. I felt as if there were those watching from past generations. A question came to my mind. "What will be the outcome of this white man's visit?" History is waiting for a generation to admit the madness of it all. Two sessions of Congress have failed to pass a resolution of apology to the native people. I have personally visited a number of congressional leaders in Washington, D.C. in attempts to garner support to pass the resolution. For the most part, those I talked to did not see the need to deal with the past. I wonder what lies ahead for a nation built on such a weak foundation. A nation that corporately cannot find the words, "We are sorry."

Nan-ye-hi might not have ever worshiped in a church. Scripture challenges us that authentic relationship is evident by visible fruit of the outward life we lead. Could it be there are many expressions of a life in Christ free from the label of savagery or paganism? Nan-ye-hi lived a Creator God dominated life; she lived in a Creator God dominated society. Subsequent to her life, her nation would not allow national office to be held by anyone who did not uphold these truths. Can you hear the Cherokee singing their unofficial national anthem "Amazing Grace" from their death march called the Trail of Tears? Many generations of little children will peep from the weeds of their exile and view their inheritance from the land cut down and rotting in the sun. When they ask their mothers, "Who did this?" they will say, "The white people did it, the Christians did it, all for cursed mammon's sake."

Less than 5 percent of native people profess a true relationship with Christ—they see Christianity as white man's religion. Many more than this, though, offer a yes to the response of being a Christian. This yes is tempered with generations of those who have been given the choice of being seen as "civilized" Christians or being killed. Most tribal people cannot find cultural identity within traditional Roman Christendom. Roman Christendom is referring to all facets of the Christian faith currently in America; this includes everyone from Roman Catholics to the Charismatic church. May God have mercy on the genocide that has occurred under the banner of the Cross.

Fire is important to the Cherokee. Women were keepers of the fire in their homes. Each year the women ceremoniously extinguished all flame within the tribe. One of the roles of the Ghighau was to reintroduce new fire. In countless ceremonies Nan-ye-hi would have helped in rekindling the fire within her tribe. It was said that if the principle people kept the fire burning the Creator God would reveal truth. An eternal flame now burns at Red Clay, Tennessee. Red Clay was the last capital of a united tribe called the Cherokee prior to the Trail of Tears. God the Father wants us to spread truth to all people without the spin of our culture.

Let us acknowledge today through prayer:

Jesus you are part of the tribe of Judah. You are a man of color, not a white man. You wore traditional regalia (special clothing). *There was power associated with your clothing.* (The women who touched the hem of your garment.) *You celebrated the many feasts of your Father. Your tribe's calendar is kept in cycles of the moon. Your Bible is a tribal book. You celebrated your ancestors* (lineage of Christ). *Your nation was lead by tribal elders. Throughout your tribe's history, animals played important roles* (whales, lions, bears, donkeys, ravens, doves). *Your Bible celebrates the created order.* (The trees will clap their hands.)

You did nothing during your life of your own accord, but always stayed submitted to your Father's will. You used water as a sign of purification. You celebrated the land of your inheritance. You took nothing from it you did not need. Your nation fought fiercely all those who attempted to take your land from you. Your nation spared no one who lived within your enemy's camp. You upheld all your tribal laws. You upheld the strict religious practices of your tribe. Your Father held your nation accountable to past generations who did not keep their covenants. You are a person who always keeps your word. You allowed false counsel to be spoken of you, without taking revenge, for the sake of your tribe. You died a tortured death at the hands of a conquering nation to save your people. All who come to you for their salvation are not saved apart from being in-grafted into your tribe.

What will be the outcome of your visit with the life and land of Nan-ye-hi?

ENDNOTE

1. Pat Aldenman, *Nancy Ward/Dragging Canoe* (Johnson City: The Overmountain Press, 1990). Very little is written about Nancy Ward except in this one source. The Cherokee Nation's history, though, is well documented; a few recommended sources follow. Author of this chapter, Ada Winn, is a relative of Nancy Ward.

AUTHOR'S RECOMMENDED READING

Releasing Heaven on Earth by Alistair Petrie

One Church Many Tribes by Richard Twiss

You Can Feel the Mountains Tremble by Dr. Quyana Suuqiina

The Cherokee People by Thomas E. Mails.

Footsteps of the Cherokee by Vicki Rozema

chapter five

The Lady With the Lamp— Florence Nightingale

by

Michal Ann Goll

O God, Thou puttest into my heart this great desire to devote myself to the sick and sorrowful. I offer it to thee. Give me my work to do.[1]

Florence Nightingale, 1820-1910

Florence Nightingale was a truly amazing lady. She was known as "the lady with the lamp," a nickname that was given to her by British soldiers who were wounded during the Crimean War in the mid-1850s.[2] They called her this because they always saw her carrying her lamp as she walked the halls of the hospital each night. Now this name has become a symbol of all that Florence stood for—a light of care for the sick, concern for soldiers' welfare, and freedom for women to choose what kind of work they want to do.

This founder of the modern nursing profession was not the romantic, gentle, retiring Victorian woman that some people might imagine. She was a bright, tough, driven professional, who became a brilliant organizer and one of the most influential women of the 19th century.

Florence was named for the city where she was born—Florence, Italy. Her date of birth was May 12, 1820. Her wealthy parents were on a two-year-long honeymoon trip through Italy when she was born.

She spent most of her childhood on the family estates in England with her mother, Fanny, her sister, Parthenope, and her father, William. Both of the girls were taught at home by their father who was a graduate of Cambridge University. He tutored them in languages, history, and philosophy, while their mother taught them the social graces.

Florence excelled in her studies, and she was a very lively and attractive young lady. Her parents probably expected her to be a refined woman of class and distinction who would eventually marry a rich, young man—but the Lord had different plans for her.

When she was 17 years old, God spoke to her heart at Embley, the family's winter home. She wrote, "On February 7, 1837, God spoke to me and called me into His service."[3]

She felt strongly that He had given her a special mission in life. She suspected that this mission would involve helping others, something that Florence had always enjoyed doing. Often, she would care for the babies of her parents' visitors, and she would help care for caretakers on her father's estates when they got sick.

She became a single-minded young lady and even turned down offers of marriage from various suitors, including one young man for whom she felt great love. Instead of attending parties to which she was invited, she would spend her time studying health and social reforms for the poor. Her mother had a hard time with this, because such things were simply not proper for wealthy young women of her day.

Though Florence felt unworthy of the calling, she continued to pursue thoughts of helping others. Her parents did not encourage her to pursue these goals, however.

Florence had deep compassion in her heart for women and children who had to work in deplorable conditions. She was concerned about the poor in her own land and the economic and political situation in Ireland. It is clear that she cared about every social issue of her day.

She made regular visits to the sick in nearby villages and began to study the nursing systems of hospitals. Nursing wasn't really a formal profession at this time, and many of the people who helped in hospitals were prostitutes, former servicemen, and drunks. Therefore, nursing was not considered to be a noble profession.[4]

In light of this, I'm sure you can imagine how horrified Florence's parents were when she told them that she wanted to be a nurse! They tried to discourage her from going out to help the sick.

THE CALL GETS CLEARER

In the spring of 1844, Florence became convinced that her calling was to nurse the sick, but she had her own health struggles to deal with first. In 1850, her family sent her to Egypt in order to recuperate, and while she was there she kept a diary, which details her dialogue with God about His calling in her life. Some of her journal entries follow:

> *March 7, 1850*—"God called me this morning and asked me would I do good for Him, for Him alone without the reputation?"

> *March 9, 1850*—"During half an hour I had by myself in my cabin settled the question with God."

> *April 1, 1850*—"Not able to go out, but wish God to have it all His own way. I like Him to do exactly as He likes without even telling me the reason."

> *May 12, 1850*—"Today I am 30, the age [when] Christ began his mission, now no more childish things, no more love, no more marriage, now, Lord, let me think only of Thy will, what Thou wouldst me to do, oh, Lord, thy will, thy will."

> *June 10, 1850*—"The Lord spoke to me. He said, 'Give five minutes every hour to the thought of Me, couldst thou but love Me as Lizzy loves her husband, how happy wouldst thou be. But Lizzy does not give five minutes every hour for the thought of her husband, she thinks of him every minute, spontaneously."[5]

God had given Florence this time to draw closer to Him. She heard Him speaking to her, and she was ready to go forth in full-flowered compassion to help those in need.

At St. Bartholomew's Hospital in London, Florence met Elizabeth Blackwell, the first woman who ever qualified to be a physician in America. Dr. Blackwell had to overcome all kinds of opposition to enter the medical profession, and Florence was greatly impressed by her. Blackwell encouraged Florence to keep on pursuing her goals.

Eventually her father reluctantly agreed for her to train as a nurse, so, when Florence was 31 years old, she went to Kaiserwerth, Germany, in order to be trained at the Lutheran Institute of Protestant Deaconesses who were running a hospital there. Her training period lasted two years.[6]

OBEDIENCE TO THE CALL

Upon her graduation from the nurses' training that had been provided by the Protestant Deaconesses, Florence went to work at a hospital for invalid women, which was located on Harley Street in London. She was appointed as the resident lady superintendent there.

While in this position, the new nurse began to think of innovations that might be employed to help the sick. For example, she developed a system of dumbwaiters, which enabled food to be delivered directly to each floor. Previously, nurses had to carry trays of food up several flights of stairs, an exhausting experience, to be sure.

Florence Nightingale also invented and installed a system of call bells that would enable patients to ring for nursing help from their beds. The bell would sound in the corridor and the valve that was attached to it remained open, enabling the nurses to see who had called for help.

She also had the water heater for the hospital installed on the top floor so that hot water would run down, making it much more accessible to the nurses.[7]

THE CRIMEAN WAR

In March, 1853, Russia invaded Turkey. Britain and France were concerned about the rise of the Russian Empire, so they responded to the invasion by declaring war on Russia in March 1854. This was the beginning of the Crimean War.

Many soldiers had to endure great hardships as they fought in this bloody war. The death rate was very high due to wounds, typhus, cholera, malaria, and dysentery. Within a few weeks after the conflict began, 8,000 men were suffering from various diseases.

The *London Times* exposed the poor medical care that was being given to the British soldiers. This caused a public outcry for greater medical care, and Florence Nightingale responded to this need by offering her services. There was still considerable prejudice against women being involved in medicine in any capacity, so the British government officials rejected her offer at first. As time went on, however, they changed their minds, because the need was so great.

Florence was given permission to take a group of 38 nurses to the military hospitals in Turkey. When she arrived at the Barak Hospital in the suburbs of Constantinople, on November 4, 1854, Florence found the conditions totally appalling.

The doctors who were there seemed to resent having female nurses, so they said, "Don't do anything until we tell you."

Florence reported that many of the men did not have blankets or nutritious food. They were unwashed, still in their uniforms, which were "stiff with dirt and gore." Many were infested with lice, and conditions there permitted only 30 men to be bathed each day—with the same sponge! Florence calculated what this meant: each patient would get bathed only once every 80 days, and it was a very poor bath, indeed. She remarked, "Perhaps it was a blessing not to be bathed!"[8]

As the number of wounded increased, the doctors decided that they needed the new nurses after all, though they still objected to many of Nightingale's views with regard to reforming the system.

Blankets were rotting in warehouses instead of providing warmth for the men, because no one had issued the proper paperwork to allow them to be distributed to the patients. The lavatories in the hospitals had no running water and the latrines were open tubs that had to be emptied by hand, but no one ever emptied them, because no one knew which department was responsible for them.

This resulted in a foul stench wafting throughout the hospital—a sickening odor that could be smelled far outside the hospital walls, as well. The sewers did not function properly, and they were frequently backed up, spewing human waste into the hospital wards. War wounds accounted for only one death in six; most deaths were caused by diseases due to the unsanitary conditions in the hospital.

The army doctors gave the nurses five cramped rooms in which to work. They found the decaying corpse of a Russian general in one of those rooms! The central yard of the quadrangle was a virtual dump that was inhabited by rats that were darting in and out of the refuse and garbage!

Each patient received a daily ration of only one pint of water. There were no cooking facilities, and only 13 five-gallon copper pots were available for feeding 2,000 men. There were no vegetables; meat and flavored water were the ingredients of the patient's daily fare. The meat came from butchered animals, and the cooks would simply throw the meat chunks into the water, which wasn't hot enough to cook anything. The patients, therefore, had to eat raw meat!

The soldiers came into the hospital with all kinds of wounds. They were ripped, torn, and mutilated. Many of their body parts were missing, and these were replaced with filthy, blood-clotted rags. The patients were laid on broken tile floors.

Florence observed the terrible conditions but did not complain. She took the words of a verse from Proverbs to heart: *"A fool uttereth all his mind, but a wise man keepeth it in till afterwards"* (Prov. 29:11).

Sometimes the doctors wouldn't let the nurses get too involved in actual medical care, so they would spend part of their time making slings, pillows, and mattresses in their efforts to help the ill and wounded. Florence was able to obtain vegetables from the local markets, and she got portable stoves, which allowed the nurses to cook meals properly. She bought tables and screens for the hospital, and many of these things were purchased from her private funds.

CHARGE OF THE LIGHT BRIGADE

When wounded troops arrived from the Battle of Balaklava, where "the charge of the light brigade" had taken place, Florence and her nurses were ready. She wrote these words: "On Thursday last, we had 1,715 sick and wounded in this hospital (among whom were 120 cholera patients) and 650 severely wounded in the other building, called the General Hospital, of which we also have charge, when a message came to me to prepare for 510 wounded on our side of the hospital, who were arriving from the dreadful affair...at Balaklava, where were 1,763 wounded and 442 killed besides 96 officers wounded and 38 killed.... We had but half an hour's notice before they began landing the wounded. Between one and nine o'clock, we had the mattresses stuffed, sewn up, and laid down...the men washed and put to bed, and all their wounds dressed.... Twenty-four cases [died] on the day of landing. We now have four miles of beds, and not eighteen inches apart.... As I went my night-rounds among the newly-wounded that night, there was not one murmur, not one groan.... These poor fellows bear pain and mutilation with an unshrinking heroism which is really superhuman, and die, or are cut up without a complaint.... We have all the sick cookery now to do—and I have got in four men for the purpose.... I hope in a few days we shall establish a little cleanliness. But we have not a basin, nor a towel, not a bit of soap, not a broom. I have ordered three hundred scrubbing brushes."[9]

In the face of such seemingly insurmountable odds many people would have despaired. Not Florence Nightingale; she persevered in her drive, compassion, and hard labor. She was able to work with the kitchen in such a way as to accommodate those patients who had special dietary needs. She and her nurses scrubbed the wards. They washed the patients and dressed their wounds regularly, and they emptied the chamber pots daily.

Out of her own money Florence purchased 6,000 hospital gowns, 2,000 pairs of socks, and hundreds of nightcaps, slippers, plates, cups, and utensils. She hired 200 Turkish workers to restore the burned-out corridors, thus making room for an additional 800 patients.

Florence Nightingale was passionate about what she knew God had called her to do, and she moved in unfeigned compassion among the sick and dying. She became compassion in action to those in need. God wants us to do the same, to be there for those who need us and to be relentless in our efforts to help them.

She hired destitute women, many of whom were prostitutes, to serve as laundresses. She recommended that a new system, which would require each bed to have tickets that would identify the patients' names and any dietary restrictions that applied to them. She wanted every patient to have his own bed with proper bedding.

Sometimes she would write letters home in behalf of the men and would send their meager wages to their families. Previously, many of them would squander their wages on alcohol. The army actually cut their wages when they got sick, and Florence assumed the role of their advocate in this matter as well as many others.

She introduced reading rooms into the hospital and secured the services of schoolmasters to give lectures to the men. Attendance at these lectures usually caused the halls to overflow.

One night, as Florence carried her lamp while doing her regular rounds, she found a man who was lying in the corridor. She realized that this soldier had never been attended to at all. In all the confusion he had been missed and now he lay there dying. He could not make a sound, and she noticed that a bullet had penetrated one of his eyes. She later wrote, "Praise God! I found a surgeon, and the surgeon was able to save him."[10]

Awhile later, as she was out on the battlefield, she saw this man again. He had recuperated from the trauma and was back fighting on the field. He brought Florence a bouquet of flowers.

Whenever she went out among the men, they would rally around her. To them she was a true heroine, for she had given dignity, care, and honor to them. One of them said, "Behold the heroic daughter of England, a soldier's friend."

Florence responded to this accolade with these words, "Give God the praise."[11]

This valiant nurse had raised the image of the British soldier from a brawling low-life to a heroic working man.

Many days she would spend eight hours on her knees dressing wounds and comforting men who were scheduled for surgery. She had a wonderful presence about her that imparted peace to their hearts and calmed their nerves. She personally ministered to at least 2,000 patients during the Crimean War.[12]

The mortality rate, which had been extremely high in the Barak Hospital, went below 10 percent under her care. Sometimes, though, Florence herself worked so hard that she would pass out from sheer exhaustion. She always got back on her feet again, though, and continued her important service to the British soldiers.

When she had to return to England due to exhaustion and illness, Florence wrote these words about her service: "Oh, my poor men who endured so patiently, I feel I have been such a bad mother to you, to come home and leave you lying in your Crimean grave. Seventy-three percent in eight regiments during six months, from disease alone, who thinks of that now? But if I could carry any one point which would prevent any part of the recurrent of this, our colossal calamity, then I should have been true to the cause of those brave dead."[13]

She had worked so hard that she suffered from extreme exhaustion, and this led to a serious, long-lasting illness. She developed a fever that was so high that the doctors had to shave her head in an effort to help release the heat from her body. For two weeks she suffered from a delirium and bone-aching pain. She couldn't get out of bed, and this frustrated her greatly because she continued to sense the need of "her men."

By this time Florence Nightingale was famous and even Queen Victoria worried about the state of her health. Eventually Florence was able to return to the hospital in Turkey, where she remained until the war was over. The conflict lasted two years and four months.

Four months after the peace treaty was signed, Florence returned home again. She hid herself away from the public, because she didn't want any of the praise that she strongly felt belonged to God. About her service during the war and her feelings about longevity she said, "It matters little provided we spend our lives to God, whether like our blessed Lord's they are concluded in three and thirty years, or whether they are prolonged to old age."

A WORKER APPROVED

Paul, in writing to Timothy, urged, *"Study and be eager and do your utmost to present yourself to God approved (tested by trial), a workman who has no cause to be ashamed, correctly analyzing and accurately dividing [rightly handling and skillfully teaching] the Word of Truth"* (2 Tim. 2:15).

Florence Nightingale was such a worker. She had studied, was eager, and certainly did her utmost to present herself to God as one who was approved. She had been tested by trial and had no reason to be ashamed. Through her marvelous example we can learn so much, because she showed us what it means to be a worker approved by God.

After the war she got involved in several things, including writing, even though she was never completely well again and was often confined to her room. Nonetheless, she was a national heroine, and she began a campaign to improve the quality of care in military hospitals.

In October 1856, she had a long interview with Queen Victoria and her husband, Prince Albert.

In 1859 she published two books that gave her opinions about the need for reform in hospital care: *Notes on Hospital* and *Notes on Nursing*. She raised funds to support her campaign to improve the quality of nursing.

In 1860, when the Civil War was beginning in America, Florence founded the Nightingale School and Home for Nurses at St. Thomas's Hospital. She also became involved in the training of nurses for employment in workhouses.

This valiant woman addressed the subject of women's rights in her book, *Suggestions for Thought to Searchers After Religious Truths*. In this work she argued for the removal of restrictions that prevented women from having careers.

Another book she wrote was entitled *Suggestions for Thought: an Address to the Artisan of England*, which she kept revising until it seemed that God had spoken to her. He said, *"You are here to carry out My program. I am not here to carry out yours."* About this word from the Lord she wrote, "I must remember that God is not my private secretary!"

She served on the Indian Sanitary Commission by gathering documentation relating to the health and sanitary administration of the army in India. Her conclusion was that the death toll from disease in the Indian army was appallingly high, with 69 out of 1,000 dying annually due to a lack of sanitation.[14] Her findings resulted in the formation of the Army Medical College.

She revolutionized the public health system of India without ever leaving England by writing pamphlet after pamphlet in which she used pie graphs to point out the most frequent causes for disease and death. She may well have been the first person to use such graphic displays to show statistics to people in an easy-to-understand manner. She was always careful to document her research.

Florence went on to study new designs for modern hospitals all over Europe. In Paris she found a revolutionary design in which separate units or pavilions made up one large hospital, and each pavilion was a light and airy, self-contained unit. This design helped to minimize infections among the patients.

She began an anthology of mystical writings, which she called, *Notes From Devotional Authors of the Middle Ages.* She believed that mystical prayer was for everyone, not just for monks, nuns, and priests. Prayer was a vital part of life for her, as it should be for each of us, and it is clear from her writings that she relied on the power of prayer throughout her life.

She wrote the manual, *Notes for Nurses and a Set of Instructions for the Training of Nurses,* which emphasized the importance of nurses maintaining a daily schedule of prayer in their lives.

Her expertise gained her a reputation in America and Britain. The United States asked for Florence's help in establishing military hospitals for soldiers in the War Between the States; and she was the first woman to receive the Order of Merit from the British government.

Due to continued overwork, her health continued to decline and she spent the last half of her life as an invalid. When she was 65, she wrote this on Christmas Day: "Today, O Lord, let me dedicate this crumbling old woman to thee; behold, the handmaid of the Lord. I was thy handmaid as a girl, since then I have backslid."

She died at the age of 90, and asked that the epitaph on her tombstone would read simply: "FN 1820 to 1910." She said that it would be a great honor for her to be buried in a casket that would be like those in which common soldiers are buried.[15]

LIONESS AMONG WOMEN

Florence Nightingale was a lioness among women; one whose faith, strength, and courage allowed her to live a compassion-acts lifestyle wherever she went.

We find a summation of her life and philosophy in something she wrote long ago: "Life is a hard fight, a struggle, a wrestling with the Principle of Evil, hand to hand, foot to foot. Every inch of the way must be disputed. The night is given us to take breath, to pray, to drink deep at the fountain of power. The day, to use the strength which has been given to us, to go forth to work with it till the evening."

This is how compassion begins, how it grows, and how it keeps on going. So, drink deep at the fountain of power, and remember these words of Paul: *"Be strong in the Lord [be empowered through your union with Him]; draw your strength from Him [that strength which His boundless might provides]"* (Eph. 6:10).

> *Dear Heavenly Father, Teach us to put you first in all that we do. Open our hearts to serve the ones you put in our path. As we serve them, we serve you—our redeemer and our provider. May we look to you for guidance and not be satisfied with earthly wealth or status. Our strength comes from you—may we use it to further your Kingdom in our world. In Jesus name, Amen.*

ENDNOTES

1. Mary Ford-Grabowski, *Sacred Voices: Essential Women's Wisdom Through the Ages*, Testament Books, (New York, NY: Testament Books, 1994), 128.

2. Basil Miller, *Florence Nightingale: The Lady Of The Lamp: Women Of Faith* (Bethany House, 1975), 72.

3. Sam Wellman, *Florence Nightingale: Lady with the Lamp: Heroes Of The Faith*, (Uhrichsville, OH: Barbour Publishing, 1999), 58.

4. Ibid., 98.

5. Ibid., 123-127.

6. Ibid., 127.

7. Ibid., 140.

8. Ibid., 152-153.

9. Ibid., 156.

10. Ibid., 168-169.

11. Ibid., 169.

12. Ibid., 166.

13. http://justus.anglican.org/resources/bio/158.html.

14. http://www.historynet.com/magazines/british_heritage/3037636.html.

15. Ibid., 202.

chapter six

Rejected by Man,
Approved by God—Gladys Aylward

by
Michal Ann Goll

I can do all things through Christ, who strengthens me
(Philippians 4:13).

A HEART FOR CHINA

"I will be glad to be of service, Sir." She grudgingly muttered these words, despite the fact her heart was ravished from the unfortunate words spoken rather harshly from the principal of the Women's Training Center of the China Inland Mission. Gladys Aylward was 27 years old and, according to the staff of her mission preparatory school, too old to begin training to become a missionary in China. Sure, she knew her record wasn't the most impressive but she was willing to do what was needed to get to China.

China. Her heart ached for China. While working as a parlor maid, she decided to attend a religious meeting and by the end of the night, Gladys gave her heart to Jesus. And He gave it back to her with a deep-rooted love not only for Himself but also for the people of China. She read an article in a *Young Life Campaign* magazine about the millions of Chinese who had never heard of the name of "Jesus," feeling an overwhelming compassion and desire to take action.1 She tried to convince some her Christian friends and relatives to take on the cause but no one seemed very concerned. Surely if she offered her assistance to her brother, he would understand her concern and move to China. Instead, he bluntly replied, "Not me! Why don't *you* go?"

Good question. Why *didn't* she go? If no one else would travel thousands of miles to a country she knew practically nothing of, she would be forced to go herself. She was told she needed to enlist in a certain missionary society and after completing training, she would be sent as a missionary to China. And now, sitting in the office of the man she hoped would help fulfill her dreams, she was being told she was too old and too far behind the rest of the class and being offered another parlor maid position; this time caring for retired missionaries in need of a housekeeper.[2]

Questions flooded Gladys' mind. *Did I do something to upset God? Do I even hear God? Maybe I'm not called to China at all....*

Shaking off these ridiculous thoughts, she held on to what she knew. God longed to embrace the Chinese people, and He wanted to use Gladys' hands and feet to do it. And in the meantime, if God wanted to use her hands and feet to serve an older missionary couple, who was she to stand in the way?

EARLY MISSIONS WORK

During Gladys' time in Bristol, England, caring for Dr. and Mrs. Fisher, she learned many valuable lessons from the couple's simple, extravagant faith in Jesus. While Gladys enjoyed the stories that filled the small house, she still longed to go and love the people of China. She moved from Bristol to work for the Christian Association of Women and Girls where she worked as a rescue sister. Each night she waded through the dark, gloomy streets near the docks, looking for girls that the sailors had made drunk, and she took them back to the hostel. While she did enjoy this work and knew God was using her, the faces of her people of China were etched in her heart and mind. She went to London to inquire of families in need of childcare—anything to make a way for her to China. The responses she found were anything but helpful. Still, she refused to lose hope.

CONFIRMATION IN SCRIPTURE

Diving into the Word for encouragement, she found herself under great conviction for her lack of faith and action concerning China. If she was so confident God had called her to China, why didn't she act on it?

She read the story of Abraham. *"Now the Lord had said unto Abram, Get thee out of thy country, and from thy kindred, and from thy father's house, unto a land that I will show thee: and I will...make thy name great; and thou shalt be a blessing"* (Gen. 12:1-2 KJV). Then she read about Moses' raw faith to obey God, and defy the might of Egypt and the despotism of Pharaoh. He just started out on the journey through the desert to reach his destiny. Nehemiah's life called out to her. She saw that not only was he a butler of sorts and had to obey his employer, like she did—but he went! She heard a clear voice speak inside her soul asking if her God was the same one as the God of Nehemiah or not. God was building a whole series of confirmations that released a surge of courage that raced through her mind and spirit.[3] The issue was settled as far as she was concerned. She knew she had received her marching orders from Heaven!

THE JOURNEY

Just as quickly as Gladys' heart surrendered to God's heart; provision and direction followed. She moved to London and began to save money for a ticket to China. But when Gladys arrived at Muller's Shipping Agency, she discovered the difficulty was not only in the price of the ticket but in the journey itself. The cheapest ticket would take her by rail through Europe, Russia, and Siberia to Tientsin in Northern China. At the time, war was raging between Russia and China. Fighting was over Manchurian soil and there was no guarantee she would get through safely. The clerk at the desk insisted traveling that distance was too great a risk, but Gladys knew in her heart she had to follow the heart of her God. And that journey led to China.

Against the advice of the clerk on duty, she opened an account with the Muller's Shipping Agency with a deposit of 3 pounds toward a ticket to China, leaving 44 pounds and ten shillings yet to pay. Within a few months, God had provided enough funds for her to travel to China. She worked extra hours, often taking on special socials and dinners. At one of these meetings, Gladys was introduced to a lady who shared interest in China and told Gladys of her friend, Mrs. Lawson, an elderly missionary in need of younger bones to carry on her work. Gladys immediately wrote to Mrs. Lawson, offering her hands. After a long wait, a reply arrived. If Gladys could travel to Tientsin, Mrs. Lawson would meet her. It was time.

She left Liverpool with a two old battered suitcases which contained, among other things, a bedroll, a small spirit stove, canned fish, crackers, boiled eggs, instant coffee, baked beans, and lots of tea. She tied on the outside of the suitcase a large pot and a kettle. She wore a bright orange dress and a huge fur overcoat with the sleeves cut out. Under her clothes she wore one of her mother's old corsets, and had sown secret pockets inside to carry her train tickets, passport, a fountain pen, her money (which was a grand nine pennies and two one-pound notes), and her Bible.[4] How she had waited for this day to come! As the train jolted across the tracks, the day turned to night and the night back into day and Gladys' excitement slowly dwindled into sadness and nervousness. She knew no one. She had no money. She was already tired.[5] What exactly was she thinking when this seemed like such a good idea?

She crossed the border into Manchuria and discovered fighting had intensified, blocking a crucial junction where Gladys had to change trains. After several stops, the lights in the train blackened and thundering gunfire broke the silence. She quickly grabbed her belongings and climbed onto the station platform, shivering in the bitter cold. The station seemed deserted; except for a few guards and uniformed officials who informed her she must walk though the howling wind and stinging cold to Chita, the previous stop on her route.

Gladys walked for several days to arrive back in Chita, stopping only to nap and nibble on the few crackers she managed to save from the train. When she arrived in Chita, officials questioned her and attempted to persuade her to stay and work in Russia. While sitting in the train station, alone and cold, she questioned God and her own sanity for venturing this journey alone, wondering if it would ever be worth it. But when she looked over and saw 50 people chained together by their hands and feet and being dragged onto trains to be taken to forced labor camps in Siberia, she knew her answer.

Of course it was worth it. She would pay any price and endure any suffering to get to China, the land where her heart longed to be so she could lavish hungry souls with the love of Jesus. With renewed energy and determination, she trekked on. After another detour, she found herself in Vladivostok where an interpreter stole her passport and, with a manipulative smile and friendly voice, offered her a decent place to stay in a nearby hotel and a tour around the city. Honored and appreciative at first, after a few days she began to feel anxious and ready to continue her journey to China. Unfortunately, the interpreter disagreed and insisted she stay and since he still had her passport, she ultimately had no choice.

Leaving the hotel in frustration, a girl appeared from behind the door and summoned her aside. In a hushed voice, the mysterious woman informed Gladys that the man who seemed hospitable had no plans of allowing Gladys to leave Russia and instructed her to quickly gather her things and wait for an old man to arrive at her door.

When a knock came a few hours later, Gladys jumped to her feet, anxious and nervous to open the door. The interpreter stood in the doorway, her passport in hand and grim expression on his face. She grabbed the passport and slammed the door shut, just in time. Looking at her passport, she saw it now read *Gladys Aylward, British subject; Profession: machinist!* The mysterious woman was telling the truth, the interpreter had tried to change Gladys passport to force her to stay in Russia.

Gladys was overwhelmed with gratitude for the angel God had sent to help her but she knew she was not safe until she was out of Russia. In the early morning, another knock came at the door. An old man stood silently and held out his hand to carry Gladys suitcase, leading her down a dark alley to the docks where they met the mysterious woman from the previous night. Again, her instructions were short and simple. Gladys must go down to the captain's hut and beg and plead, whatever it takes, to get on the boat for Japan.

With no valuables or money, Gladys only had one thing to offer the captain as a bargain: herself. Gladys agreed to become his prisoner, as long as they left Russia.[6]

In the darkest hour, Gladys knew she had a choice. She could forget why she had traveled such a dangerous journey and become consumed with hopelessness and sadness at the terrible situation or she could choose to believe. And she knew she must choose to believe in the goodness and faithfulness of her precious God and faithful King.

TOUCHING THE SOIL

Eventually the boat reached Japan and she found herself in the hands of the British Consulate. Relieved by the familiar voices and comforting words of the officials, she was filled with joy and comfort. God was so faithful! He had once again delivered her from the enemy's hands and placed her in safe territory. On Sunday, November 5, 1932, three weeks after her departure from London, she stepped on her last train ride into Tientsin to finally meet Mrs. Lawson. Her heart fell in love with the beautiful countryside, high mountains with snow-covered tops and bright green and red trees. Three days later, her feet touched the soil of a land she immediately called home.

China.

THE BEGINNING

When Gladys arrived in China, exhausted and dirty, she was relieved the journey was complete but nervous about the long-awaited meeting with Mrs. Lawson. Feeling unworthy and insignificant, much due to her unsightly appearance, she once again realized she had only one thing to offer: herself.

Mrs. Jeannie Lawson was from Scotland and rarely showed any sign of emotion. Rather harshly, Gladys was ushered into what was soon to be her new home. Gladys realized her hopes for a comfortable bed and warm bath were a bit premature when she walked into a partially dilapidated house where a cement floor was her bed. When asked where she should change clothes, Mrs. Lawson politely told her to sleep in her clothes with all her belongings within hands reach—having her things close made them harder to steal. Gladys couldn't hide her frustration and angst and again began questioning her sanity for her move to China. Apparently, the news of her arrival had spread around town and she awoke with dozens of faces peering into the open windows. At any rate, she was at least grateful for the advice of Mrs. Lawson to sleep in her clothes!

Gladys was surprised at the bleak and poor conditions she and Mrs. Lawson faced on a daily basis. Ministry was not glamorous, she realized. Mrs. Lawson had little money, Gladys had nothing. So when Mrs. Lawson informed Gladys of her plans to transform the house into a working inn, Gladys was indeed relieved to know another source of income was on the way.

WORKING WITH MULES

The inn was in Yangcheng, a little Chinese village in the country that sat on the ancient mule track where muleteers, the newsmen of North China, would travel on a regular basis. Excited about the opportunity to love and minister the good news of Jesus to the muleteers, Gladys was less than thrilled when she was assigned her task. Her job was to stand in the streets and when the mules started to pass, grab its head and drag him inside. Apparently, once this is done the rest of the mules follow and the muleteers would stay in the inn.

On her first day, Gladys stood shaking with fright as she waited for the mules to pass. Her first attempt failed miserably; the owner was so frightened he ran away! But soon Gladys perfected "the grab" and their home became known along the route as a clean inn where the foreign ladies told long stories at night, free of charge. The nighttime was Gladys' favorite part of the day because it was during these late hours Mrs. Lawson would begin to tell wonderful stories of their sweet Jesus. Gladys would listen carefully, trying to learn the language from Mrs. Lawson's stories, longing for the day it would be her turn to share.

Gladys completed all her daily tasks, no matter how miniscule they seemed, to the best of her ability, knowing God could use even the smallest deeds of the day to His glory. She followed Mrs. Lawson faithfully, doing just as she was instructed and using any opportunity to learn more of her language. Days were often spent cleaning and during the night, Gladys could usually be found outside cleaning and caring for the mules.

TWO WOMEN IN CHINA

On weekends the duo would travel to villages, wait until crowds gathered to gaze in curiosity at the foreign ladies and begin to preach the Gospel. The villagers would stare in amazement as some had never before seen a white person, especially at their feet. A Chinese custom required all women to have their feet bound so Mrs. Lawson and Gladys' free feet always brought much attention.

Mrs. Lawson and Gladys were indeed a unique pair. Gladys' youthful energy was a definite contrast to the elderly Mrs. Lawson, strong in heart but growing weaker by the day. But what did unite the two was an unshakeable, firm belief that God had called them to China; their love for the Chinese people was strong enough to fill any gap. Gladys often wondered what would happen if Mrs. Lawson died, if she would be sent back to London or if she would venture on alone.

Later on in the year, while Gladys was away from the inn, Mrs. Lawson had a terrible accident, having fallen from the second story balcony, and had lain outside for over a week, exposed to the weather, without any assistance from anyone. When Gladys returned, she found dear Mrs. Lawson lying on top of a pile of coal, where she had fallen. Gladys cared for her, and nursed her, but it became evident she was not going to recover. Shortly before she graduated to be with Jesus, Mrs. Lawson whispered to Gladys, "God called you to my side, Gladys, in answer to my prayers. He wants you to carry on my work here. He will provide. He will bless and protect you."[7] Mrs. Lawson's funeral was the first Christian burial ever to be held in Yangcheng.[8]

LAUNCHING OUT

Now being alone, Gladys kept the inn running and held Gospel meetings in the evenings. She traveled around villages, caring for and giving medical aid as best she could. Funds were extremely low, but that wasn't all. Mrs. Lawson had never told Gladys about a yearly tax, due to the mandarin. This was a large amount, which Mrs. Lawson had paid out of her small monthly income. Now, those funds were no longer available, and the payment was due! Alone and tired, Gladys wondered how the she would meet the needs of her workers, her guests, and her beloved Chinese people. She felt weak and helpless, knowing God must truly work a miracle if she were to continue her work in China. Unable to bear the thought of closing the inn and leaving China, she knew the only place to go was to the feet of her Jesus and offer the only thing she had to give: herself.

She thought perhaps she should go and bow before the mandarin, but this idea presented several problems. Since Mrs. Lawson and Gladys were the first two foreigners to live in Yangcheng, there were no set rules as to how many times one should bow to the mandarin, or what she should say, or in what order either of these things should be done. Making just one mistake pertaining to proper protocol could be deadly, as the mandarin was the highest official in the district. The more she thought about this idea, the more she realized it just wouldn't be appropriate. She did not have any clothes suitable to seek an audience, having only her quilted blue trousers and jacket. No, there had to be some other way to deal with paying the taxes.

UNEXPECTED TURN OF EVENTS

About a week later, Gladys had a very unexpected surprise. The mandarin was seen coming to the inn. *What could be the problem? Had she done something wrong?* There was no time to make any preparations, she would just have to receive him with all the honor she held in her heart, and hope it would make the difference.

She bowed twice and waited, but the mandarin seemed focused on a mission. As he began speaking with her, the reason for his visit became clear. A new government had been formed in Nanking, and they had established a new law. This law addressed the ancient custom of foot binding.

This custom was employed as women with small feet were considered the ultimate in sexual appeal. The eligibility for a good marriage depended solely on this criteria in those days. Chinese families, depending on how affluent they were, would bind the feet of their girl children between the ages of three to seven years. As the bones in a little child's feet are soft and pliable, the little girls' feet were wrapped tight with linen bandages. The feet would slowly double over until the toes and front half of the foot were tucked underneath. By the time a girl was 12 or 13 years old, her feet would be permanently doubled in half.

Those who were less wealthy held off this custom for as long as they could so that their daughter could be useful longer around the house and the fields. Once her feet were bound, she would have difficulty getting around. Presumably, it insured that the woman would remain mainly confined to the home and depend solely on her husband also ensuring that this way she would remain chaste, thus making it very popular.[9]

The new law required the mandarin to retain a foot inspector. This, in itself, had two obstacles. First, it could not be a man, as men were not allowed to look at a woman's feet. That meant the inspector had to be a woman. But, all the women had their feet bound and would not be able to travel on foot over mountains and rough roads to reach all the villages. These two issues narrowed down his search to the woman now standing in front of him. Who else was there who spoke the Yangcheng dialect and had unbound feet, and was a woman? There was only one; it was Gladys, in the entire Yangcheng district. She had made herself available, and now God was about to open to her a large field, ready to be harvested!

The mandarin offered to pay her for this service, which would take care of the needed monies for the taxes. This would give her opportunity to tell every village about Jesus, throughout the entire district, besides getting to help enforce the end of this terrible, torturous custom.

She found herself replying to him that if she took on this responsibility of representing his excellency, that she would speak of the love of God to everyone, and lead as many to Jesus as she could. After thinking a few minutes, he in turn responded that if the women became Christians, they would want their daughters to have unbound feet like Gladys, and that would be a good thing.

This audience, which only took a few minutes, was the beginning for what would later become a crucial piece for the complete fulfillment of God's purposes in Gladys' life. As she went from village to village, house to house, she gathered each little girl in her arms, unbound the little feet which had turned white from lack of blood, and of which the girl's toes were already folded over. She gently massaged the feet until a pink color began to return and the toes began to uncurl, and then soundly threatened that if she came back and found the girl's feet bound again, that person would surely be put in prison! Many times she would be invited to the home of the elder of the village where she would spend the night, and tell stories of Jesus, her wonderful friend and Saviour!

SENT OUT

After several months, she had reached every village, every family, and unbound every girl's foot. She reported to the mandarin her progress, and he urged her to continue her rounds, making sure everyone was complying. Once the girls' feet were unbound, the parents often decided they were glad the old custom was abolished. This freed Gladys' time so that as she traveled, she was able to spend her time telling the people about Jesus. The villagers anticipated her visits, and as time passed, small bands of Christians began forming in the villages. Gladys visited the mandarin regularly, giving him updates on the region. He was greatly impressed with her work.

THE NEXT ASSIGNMENT

Some time later, another task was assigned to the "foot inspector." This time inmates in the prison had started a riot. They were killing each other. The mandarin, not knowing anyone else with as much courage or ability, summoned Gladys to the prison. Feeling totally overwhelmed and unprepared to face murderers and robbers, once she reluctantly arrived at the prison, she argued with the governor of the prison. *What did she know about fighting, herself being a woman! Surely she would be killed!*

The governor looked at her, and smilingly told her that she had been telling everyone that the living God lived inside her, so how could anyone kill her? Faced with the realization that this was the moment of truth, and that she had to stand on her faith in God, she silently prayed for God's protection and strength. She walked through the iron gate and down the pitch-black tunnel into the prison courtyard. She saw blood splattered everywhere as men lay dead or dying all over the ground. Men were running around with machetes, attacking each other.

CHANGING THE ATMOSPHERE

Into this den of violence, anger and hate, Gladys stepped out of the shadows, and ordered the men to stop at once, and hand over the weapons, come together and clean up the mess they had created. As she talked with them, she saw the desperation they were living in. They're bodies were so very thin with oozing, open sores all over, lice in their hair, everywhere, and what clothing they owned was completely worn out.

The men were dependent on their relatives to bring them food—if they had no relatives, well, there was no food supplied for them. Gladys heard the stories of their situation and determined in her heart to do something about it. *Who wouldn't riot living in such conditions!* She corrected the governor of the prison, and told him things could not stay the way they were. She arranged for two old looms to be brought in so the prisoners could weave their own clothes, local merchants supplying yarn. She begged for a miller's wheel so they could grind their own grain, and she taught the men how to breed rabbits for sale.

Within a few months of the riot, the men were dressed warmly and eating well. They gave her a new name; Ai-weh-deh, which means virtuous one. Soon the name caught on, and everyone was calling her by her new name.

SERVING THE CHILDREN

As her understanding of the culture in this region grew, Ai-weh-deh became aware of the trade of buying and selling children. Her heart was continually being enlarged with every plight she discovered. *How could she leave these little ones to suffer when she could do something on their behalf!* One by one, she began adopting children. The first was Ninepence, followed by Less, Boa-Boa, Francis, and Lan Hsiang. Having adopted these children, she felt she needed to become a Chinese citizen, so she would never be separated from them. The mandarin helped her fill out many papers, and in 1936 Gladys Aylward became the first foreign missionary to become a Chinese citizen.

The mandarin came to her regularly for help in solving problems. She started a school at the request of the prison governor. These were days of fulfillment and becoming really established in the region. However there was a shadow of a problem in the distance that would soon knock on her door. War was about to envelope Yangcheng.

EFFECTS OF WAR

The Japanese had invaded Manchuria and set up their government there. But now they were moving further into northeastern China. Suddenly one morning in the spring of 1938, their beloved village was bombed. Very few even knew what a bomb was! The town was totally devastated. The streets had huge craters in them, shops and houses were just piles of rubble. People were in shock.

Gladys gathered everyone together and set everyone to work. Gladys worked long hours caring for the wounded, when suddenly she realized the mandarin was standing over her head. He brought word to her that the Japanese were only about two days away from Yangcheng. The destruction that lay around them was only the beginning.

Several years of conflict between Japan and China followed. The conflict weakened the Chinese nationalist government to such an extent that the Communist government was able to slowly gain strength. During these years regions went back and forth between Chinese and Japanese control.

Yangcheng was emptied on different occasions. The first time, under the counsel of Gladys, the prison governor, and the mandarin, everyone was told to leave the village, take their food and livestock, giving the Japanese no reason to stay. Gladys, because of her extensive travels throughout the region, knew a perfect hiding place—Bei Chai Chuang. It was ideal as there was no road that led to it, it was not on any map, and most importantly, the surrounding hills housed several large caves that were almost impossible to spot from the outside. This would become home to Gladys and her children for some time. Local people brought in food and supplies. A slow trickle of sick and wounded found their way to Gladys, knowing she would care for them. The cave was transformed into a hospital.

Things seemed to settle down in the beginning days of 1939, some things almost seeming normal. But once again, the Japanese were on the move and this time the Chinese felt the best way to defend the land was what they called a "scorched earth policy"—leave nothing, no food, no crops, no buildings intact—everything was destroyed or burned. The people of China would be left with nothing!

A FEAST TO HONOR

On the eve before all was destroyed, the mandarin held one last feast at his home and invited Gladys to attend. She was given the seat of honor. All the important people of Yangcheng were there. The mandarin stood to his feet, and spoke of the many things Ai-weh-deh had done for him, and for the people, going on for more than 20 minutes. Finally, at the end of his speech, he looked her very directly in the eye, called her his dear friend, and told her he had seen all she was and all that she did. He wanted to become a Christian like her. All Gladys could think of was how grateful she was to the Lord, that He would do such a work in the mandarin's heart!

PLACES OF HIDING

The war went on and on, and the scorched-earth policy left many in need. The caves continued to be a place of safety, and many came across the kindness and care of Gladys. When the number of children flooding in reached 150, Gladys stopped trying to keep count of them all. She endured many close calls with the Japanese. She ran through gun fire, wormed her way through wheat fields to escape, traveled along danger-ous mountain trails, hiding in clefts of rocks through the night, endured the butt of a rifle on the side of her head, from which she never fully recovered.

She traveled from village to village, encouraging the churches there. Because of her extensive knowledge of the area, the general of the Chinese army requested any troop movement information she could give him. She was glad to do this, and knew she had become a spy for the land she loved. In the midst of all of this, she just kept doing what she could, many times not knowing if she would succeed. One of the prayers she had learned from Mrs. Lawson was, "If I die, let me not be afraid of death, but let there be a meaning, O God, in my dying."

"WANTED"

She was interviewed by an American freelance journalist named Theodore White around 1940-1941. Her story was so compelling; it was published in *Time* magazine and was read by millions of people, which unfortunately included the Japanese army. This ended up endangering her life, and those under her care, as the Japanese put her on their wanted list—offering $100 dead or alive![10]

TWO HUNDRED-MILE JOURNEY

A possible connection came up in regard to providing care for the 200 children now in her care. It would require dividing them into two groups, and sending each group on a 200-mile journey, across the Yellow River to Sian in Shensi province. The first group, led by one of the new converts made it safely, but on his way back to get the second group of children, this new convert, named Tsin Pen-kuang, was captured by the Japanese, robbed and killed. The Time magazine article, by this time, had fallen into Japanese hands. Now, the remaining children were at greater risk, just being with her. *What should she do? What could she do?*

"Flee ye! Flee ye into the mountains! Dwell deeply in the hidden places, because the King of Babylon has conceived a purpose against you!" Her eyes read the verses from her Chinese Bible. Now she knew what she was to do! She gathered all the children together, and put on every piece of clothing they had and tied around their waists every spare pair of shoes they could find. Their shoes were made of cloth and would barely last a day on the rugged trails they would climb. Everyone had to carry their own bedroll. The oldest children were around 15 years old, the youngest were barely 4 years of age. She wrapped all the food she had in a rag, barely enough millet for two days rations, and she carried the old iron pot herself, to cook the millet in. No one had any idea how long a journey they were embarking on.

They slept in Buddhist temple courtyards, in the open air, in small homes, wherever they could find shelter. The older girls, whose feet had been bound previously, had great difficulty, because of the weakness and abnormal bone formation. Finding enough food to feed 100 children every day was more than just a challenge. They trekked over mountains with bruised and cut feet, the younger children in great despair, crying for lack of food and being afraid. Gladys herself was dealing with a strange tiredness, a result of the rifle blow to her head. She had to keep going!

Sometimes they sang hymns; sometimes they were silent, except for the children crying. There were many Japanese in the area, and they always had to be on the lookout—not knowing what they would do if they ran into any of them. There were the soldiers on the ground, but also they had to watch out for the Japanese war planes, that could suddenly appear. At times, they ran into Chinese soldiers, who sometimes carried sugar treats and food the children had not seen for months in Shansi province.

The soldiers were glad to share their provisions, missing their own beloved children. As food supplies dwindled, they picked twigs and leaves and brewed "tea"—anything to fill all the hungry stomachs. They had to cross the Yellow River, but when they arrived she noticed that everyone had fled and there was no way to cross—all of the boats were gone. They sat by the river four days before a Chinese soldier overheard them singing. There was one boat available to ferry the children across, but it would be very dangerous. If a Japanese war plane happened over the area at the wrong time, all would be lost. Gladys was slipping in and out of consciousness. Trying to stand made her feel dizzy. They prayed and after three trips across the river—all were safely on the other side. Relief was close at hand now—or was it?

The next morning they boarded the train, rode for three days only to discover the bridge had been blown out. To get to Sian, they would have to climb over another mountain, and catch another train on the other side. It would take four or five days to make this leg of the journey. *How were they going to make it?*

They got off the train and gazed at the steep grade of the climb before them. Gladys sat down on a rock and just started to cry. One by one, they all joined in and cried together for several minutes till Gladys stopped, wiped her eyes on her sleeve and told the children it was okay to cry, but now it was time to move. It was time to sing, and time to march!

At every promise of being "almost there," there was always further to go it seemed, more miles to walk, "this train can't carry passengers; you can't stop here; no more refugees are being accepted"—the delays were many. Finally, after three weeks or more, they arrived at Fufeng, a city that was still receiving refugees.

By this point Gladys, who didn't know it at the time, was suffering from fever, pneumonia, typhoid, and malnutrition. She delivered safely every child, not one of them had died or become seriously ill. She hardly knew who or where she was, and two days after getting the children to safety in an orphanage, she fell into a coma that lasted two weeks.

NEED FOR REST

It was time for recuperation. Gladys would require much time. She got stronger, and was able to resume her missionary work. She visited the head lama in Tibet, who told her they had been waiting for three years for someone to come who could tell them more about God. He showed her the Scripture, John 3:16: *"For God so loved the world that He gave His only begotten Son."* which had been glued to the wall. She preached to the 500 Lamaist monks and prayed with them. She worked in a leper colony and preached in a local prison. Everywhere she went; many Chinese people were searching for the one true God.

She witnessed among university students the ugliness of the communist regime, as they were given the choice to either support the communist government, or not. One by one, these fiery students, who knew of a higher allegiance, after having made their declaration for Jesus, were promptly shoved to their knees and beheaded, right there on the spot.

BACK TO ENGLAND

Gladys went back to England for awhile; to recoup some more from the physical rigors she had endured. She was not prepared for how famous she had become. She traveled many places, using her notoriety to call Christians to pray for China, and send relief to the Chinese people. Hollywood made a movie about her life called, "Inn of the

Sixth Happiness" and the big London newspapers interviewed her. She was introduced to heads of state, and met Queen Elizabeth, and worked with the many refugees who streamed into England.[11]

DESIRE TO GO HOME

After ten years in England, she traveled back "home." Entry into mainland China was not allowed, and her Chinese citizenship was not honored at this time, so in 1957 she landed in Formosa (modern-day Taiwan). She picked up her life where she had left off. Her heart was full, and her hands were never empty.

HER LAST DAY

On New Year's Day in 1970, Gladys simply did not wake up. She was 67 years old, and her heart just stopped beating. Beside her bed was a newborn baby, sleeping peacefully. The baby had been abandoned, and brought to Ai-weh-deh. The baby was received with open, loving arms.

Memorial services were held around the world for this amazing woman, and over 1,000 people attended her funeral service Taipei. Gladys' body was buried on a hilltop at Christ's College in Taipei; her tomb faces the Chinese mainland.

If ever I heard a trumpet sound from a single voice—this trumpet is still blasting, this voice is still singing, "All for Jesus, I surrender...I surrender all!"

I believe I hear another voice singing the same song—we know her as Mother Teresa.

Father, We come to you in the name of Jesus. We pray that we would know your voice and your Word so well, that we would be totally transformed by your Word, and become living epistles to the world you are sending us to. Oh Lord, may we be so in love with you, that no obstacle would keep us from doing all we can do, for your name's sake. May man's opinion not sway or affect our focus and determination to do all you have deposited in our hearts. May we always remember that it is your approval, not man's, that counts! In Jesus name, Amen.

ENDNOTES

1. Janet and Geoff Benge, *Gladys Aylward: The Adventure of a Lifetime, Christian Heroes: Then & Now*, (YWAM Publishers, 1998), 170.

2. Ibid., 20-21.

3. Gladys Aylward as told to Christine Hunter, *Gladys Aylward: The Little Woman*, (Moody Publishers, 1974), 10-12.

4. Janet and Geoff Benge, *Gladys Aylward*, 33.

5. Sam Wellman, *Gladys Aylward: Missionary to China: Heroes Of The Faith* (Barbour Publishing, 1998), 34.

6. Gladys Aylward, *Gladys Aylward*, 31.

7. Ibid., 42.

8. Janet and Geoff Benge, *Gladys Aylward*, 104.

9. http://www.globalartmall.com/2006/02/chinese-foot-bind ing_13.html.

10. Janet and Geoff Benge, *Gladys Aylward*, 169.

11. Ibid., 201.

chapter seven

The Humble Road—Mother Teresa

by
Michal Ann Goll

In the slums we are the light of God's kindness to the poor. To the children, to all who suffer and are lonely, give always a happy smile. Give them not only your care but also your heart.[1]

Mother Teresa, 1910-1997

PARAGON OF COMPASSION

If you asked people, "Who was the most compassionate person of the 20th century?" I'm sure many would answer without hesitation, "Mother Teresa." She moved in compassion among the poor in her beloved Calcutta, India, and among the rich and famous around the world, as well. She was a flesh-and-blood example of what compassion looks like, and she seemed to constantly exhibit the qualities of humility and love wherever she was.

Indeed, she obviously took joy from her service to others and this seemed to fill her heart with peace. This was reflected in her radiant, smiling countenance.

There is much we can learn from Mother Teresa, and I feel as if I have actually gotten to know her as I researched and wrote this chapter. I hope you are inspired as you read these pages about her life and ministry.

Mother Teresa of Calcutta (Agnes Gonxha Bojaxhiu) was born on August 27, 1910, in Skopje, which is in modern Macedonia. Her family was of Albanian descent, and she was the youngest of three children. Her father was a builder.

At the age of 12 Agnes strongly felt the call of God on her life, and she knew that she was destined to become a missionary. The overarching desire of her life from then on was to spread the love of Jesus Christ, particularly among the poor, the sick, and the outcasts of society. God called her and she responded with a vibrant "Yes!"

When she was 18 years old, Agnes left home to join the Sisters of Loretto, an Irish community of nuns who managed mission schools in India. As a novice in this order, she took the name of Sister Teresa. She served her novitiate in Dublin, and after several months of training she was sent to India. On May 25, 1931, she took her initial vows as a nun.

From 1931 to 1948, Sister Teresa taught at St. Mary's High School in Calcutta. While there, she was moved with deep compassion for the poor and suffering people she saw outside the walls of the convent. Thousands of destitute refugees lived there with little hope that the basic necessities of life—food, shelter, health, cleanliness, and income— would ever be theirs.

In 1946, Sister Teresa developed a suspected case of tuberculosis. Thinking that mountain air would be good for her, she took a train to the village of Darjeeling in the foothills of the Himalayas. While sitting on the train, she heard God speaking to her and telling her that He wanted her to serve Him "among the poorest of the poor."[2]

Soon thereafter she recovered from her illness and received permission to leave her order. She moved to Calcutta's slums to set up her first school for slum children in an open-air mission. She had no funds for this work, so she had to depend totally on God and launched out in faith and full trust in Him.

Clearly, she knew the truth of this Scripture: *"But without faith it is impossible to please and be satisfactory to Him; For whoever would come near to God must [necessarily] believe that God exists and that He is the rewarder of those who earnestly and diligently seek Him [out]"* (Heb. 11:6).

Before long, volunteers joined with her, and people who saw what she was doing began to provide financial support for her fledgling ministry. This allowed her work and ministry to grow.

CALCUTTA, INDIA

Calcutta (Kolkata) is the capital of the Indian state of West Bengal in eastern India. It is the fourth largest city in India, with a population that currently exceeds five million.

After India declared its independence from Great Britain in 1947, due largely to the influence of Mahatma Gandhi, the city went through an extended period of economic stagnation and many of its inhabitants were the "poorest of the poor." The city's port was bombed by the Japanese twice during World War II.

Millions starved to death during the Bengal famine of 1943. In 1946 demands for the creation of a Muslim state led to massive violence in the city, which caused the deaths of more than 2,000 people. Sister Teresa went through these great trials with the Indian people, so she knew how intense their suffering and hardships were.

In spite of its poverty, violence, and bloodshed, Calcutta came to be known as "the City of Joy," and Sister Teresa was able to help turn suffering into joy for many people who lived there.

Through you, God can do the same for others. He wants His people to know what David experienced: *"You have turned my mourning into dancing for me; You have put off my sackcloth and girded me with gladness."* (See Psalm 30:11.) This is what you and I, like Mother Teresa, can help others to discover!

When the subcontinent was divided between India and Pakistan in 1947, a flood of over one million destitute refugees poured into Calcutta. Most of these people were Hindus who had no concept of a personal God who was their heavenly Father.

The majority of people who lived in Calcutta during the 1940s lived in the worst possible conditions of extreme hunger, deprivation, squalor, and filth.

Sister Teresa gathered the city's "throwaway children" from rubbish heaps. Many were orphans. She explained, "We do our best to nurse them back to life."[3]

This valiant nun could see the life of Jesus in every child and adult, and she approached each one as if he or she was the Lord himself. She was their servant, an obedient follower of the One who said, *"For I was hungry and you gave Me food. I was thirsty and you gave Me something to drink, I was a stranger and you brought Me together with yourselves and welcomed and entertained and lodged Me. I was naked and you clothed Me, I was sick and you visited Me with help and ministering care. I was in prison and you came to see Me"* (Matt. 25:35-36).

When Jesus' disciples asked Him when it was that they had done these things, He said, *"Truly I tell you, in so far as you did it for one of the least [in the estimation of men] of these My brethren, you did it for Me"* (Matt. 25:40).

Sister Teresa gave food to the hungry, hospitality to the strangers, clothes to the naked, and healing and practical help to the ill. She knew that in doing so she was ministering to the One who loves each person equally and without partiality.

SAINT OF THE GUTTER

On October 7, 1950, Sister Teresa was given permission by the Holy See to found a new order of Catholic nuns—the Missionaries of Charity. She was now Mother Teresa of Calcutta, the Mother Superior of this new order.[4]

She saw the order's primary task as being the provision of love and care for needy persons who had no one to help them.[4] Mother Teresa described their mission as follows: "... [to care for] the hungry, the naked, the homeless, the crippled, the blind, the lepers, all those people who feel unwanted, unloved, uncared for throughout society, people that have become a burden to the society and are shunned by everyone."[5]

The Missionaries of Charity began with only 12 members in Calcutta. Today there are more than 4,000 nuns in the order throughout the world, and they minister to orphans, AIDS victims, refugees, the blind, the disabled, the aged, alcoholics, the poor, victims of natural disasters, and the hungry. The nuns can be found working in Asia, Africa, Latin America, North America, Poland, and Australia.

Mother Teresa always emphasized service to others. She believed and followed these words of Jesus: *"And whosoever of you shall be the chiefest, shall be servant of all"* (Mark 10:44 KJV). She became a leader, because she was a servant, and she and her Sisters of Charity truly were the servants of all. These are some of the reasons why Mother Teresa became known as "the saint of the gutter."

HER SPIRITUAL LIFE

Pope John Paul II admired Mother Teresa, and he said that she was one of the greatest missionaries of the 20th century. He explained, "The Lord made this simple woman who came from one of Europe's poorest regions a chosen instrument (cf. Acts 9:15) to proclaim the Gospel to the entire world, not by preaching but by daily acts of love towards the poorest of the poor. A missionary with the most universal language: the language of love that knows no bounds or exclusion and has no preferences other than for the most forsaken.... Where did Mother Teresa find the strength to place herself completely at the service of others? She found it in prayer and in the silent contemplation of Jesus Christ...."[6]

I believe the pope was exactly right about the source of Mother Teresa's strength—prayer and the contemplation of her Lord and Master, Jesus Christ. This is the same place where you and I will find the strength we need to go forth in service, as well; it is the secret place of the Most High.

In his first encyclical, Pope Benedict XVI echoed John Paul's observations by stating, "In the example of Blessed Teresa of Calcutta we have a clear illustration of the fact that time devoted to God in prayer not only does not detract from effective and loving service to our neighbour but is in fact the inexhaustible source of that service."[7]

ANGEL OF MERCY

Mother Teresa was also known as an "angel of mercy" to the poor. This is an apt description of her work, for an angel is a messenger, one who is always ready to come to the aid of others.

She opened *Nirmal Hriday* ("Pure or Immaculate Heart"), a home for the dying, in 1952. This hostel became the focal point of her ministry for a couple of years. The government leaders of Calcutta gave her the use of a building for this purpose.

Writer Eileen Egan describes her work there as follows: "I watched Mother Teresa as she sat on the parapet next to the low pallets of men, patting their heads or stroking their stick-like arms, murmuring to each one. Sometimes only the eyes seemed alive in men whose skin was drawn so tightly that the skull seemed struggling to burst through. Some were even smiling, as though amazed to be alive. It was the same in the women's hall. Seeing me, they held out their wasted hands to me, searching for human consolation.

"I turned away in fear and shame. I wondered how she could face day after day caring for those who were brought in covered with the filth and spittle of the gutter.

"Mother Teresa explained that her work and the work of the Sisters called for them to see Jesus in everyone, including the men and women dying in the gutter."[8]

Mother Teresa said that in the earlier days of their ministry they did little planning. They simply responded to the needs, and she said that God showed them what to do.

She said, "Keep giving Jesus to your people not by words, but by your example, by your being in love with Jesus, by radiating his holiness and spreading his fragrance of love everywhere you go. Just keep the joy of Jesus as your strength. Be happy and at peace. Accept whatever he gives—and give whatever he takes with a big smile. You belong to him."[9]

I love this simple statement of faith. Never forget that you are God's property, as Paul pointed out to the Corinthians: *"You were bought with a price [purchased with a preciousness and paid for, made His own]. So then, honor God and bring glory to Him in your body"* (1 Cor. 6:20).

Knowing that we are no longer our own, that we have been bought with a price, helps to clarify many things in our lives. It helps us to see what God wants us to do. It makes us realize that we do not have to do anything in our own strength.

So, surrender yourself to the One who created you and gave His life for you. Let Him live His life through you, as Mother Teresa did.

PURE RELIGION

James writes, *"External religious worship [religion as it is expressed in outward acts] that is pure and unblemished in the sight of God the Father is this: to visit and help and care for the orphans and widows in their affliction and need, and to keep oneself unspotted and uncontaminated from the world"* (James 1:27).

Mother Teresa's life was characterized by this kind of "external religious worship." Her ministry to the orphans was pure and unblemished, and she kept herself uncontaminated by the world.

After opening her free hospice for the poor, Mother Teresa opened a home for lepers, which she called *Shanti Nagar* ("City of Peace"). Then she opened an orphanage, *Shishu Bhavan.* She became a true mother to the precious children who lived there.

About her work in the orphanage, Mother Teresa wrote, "One of the abandoned children we had in our Shishu Bhavan I gave to a very high-class and rich family. After a few months I heard that the child had become very sick and completely disabled. So I went to that family and said, 'Give me back the child and I will give you a healthy child.'

"The father looked at me and said, 'Take my life first, then take the child.' He loved the child from his heart.

"In Calcutta, every night we send word to all the clinics, to all the police stations, to all the hospitals, 'Please do not destroy any children; we will take them all.'

"So our house is always full of children. There is a joke in Calcutta: 'Mother Teresa is always talking about family planning and abortion, but every day she has more and more children.'"[10]

How did Mother Teresa learn to be such a giving parent? She developed her parenting skills by getting to know her heavenly Father. She often spoke of His tenderness to her and quoted these verses from the Prophet Isaiah:

> *But now [in spite of past judgments for Israel's sins], thus says the Lord, He Who created you, O Jacob, and He Who formed you, O Israel: fear not, for I have redeemed you [ransomed you by paying a price instead of leaving you captives]; I have called you by your name; you are Mine. When you pass through the waters, I will be with you, and through the rivers, they will not overwhelm you. When you walk through the fire, you will not be burned or scorched, nor will the flame kindle upon you* (Isaiah 43:1-2).

She knew that God was her loving heavenly Father and that He would always be with her. She stood upon His promise that He would never leave her nor forsake her. It was obvious to all who knew her that she knew God personally and intimately.

Mother Teresa understood that God had adopted her into His family, that she was His child. Like Paul, she believed, *"For all who are led by the Spirit of God are sons of God. For [the Spirit which] you have now received* [is] *not a spirit of slavery to put you once more in bondage to fear, but you have received the Spirit of adoption [the Spirit producing sonship] in [the bliss of] which we cry, Abba (Father)! Father!"* (Rom. 8:14-15).

I'm sure this is why she respected life so much and was adamantly opposed to abortion. She always encouraged people to adopt children so that they could experience family love, nurturing, and support.

She frequently spoke against abortion and artificial contraception. When she accepted the Nobel Peace Prize in 1979, she said, "I feel the greatest destroyer of peace today is abortion, because it is a direct war, a direct killing—direct murder by the mother herself.... Because if a mother can kill her own child—what is left for me to kill you and you kill me—there is nothing between."[11]

To her, abortion was infanticide—a blatant disregard for God's gift of life, and in 1994, at the National Prayer Breakfast in Washington, D.C., she said, "Please don't kill the child. I want the child. Please give me the child. I am willing to accept any child who would be aborted and to give that child to a married couple who will love the child and be loved by the child."[12]

This is complete compassion—a willingness to do all that could be done for those in need. Her offer to take any unwanted child had no limits; it was an open-ended and heart-felt invitation from a true mother who knew how much Jesus loves the little children.

Her offer reminds me of what Jesus said, *"...Allow the little ones to come to Me, and do not forbid or restrain or hinder them, for of such [as these] is the kingdom of heaven composed"* (Matt. 19:14).

FORGIVENESS

Mother Teresa believed in the importance of forgiveness. She said, "I once picked up a woman from a garbage dump and she was burning with fever; she was in her last days and her only lament was: 'My son did this to me.' I begged her: 'You must forgive your son. In a moment of madness, when he was not himself, he did a thing he regrets. Be a mother to him, forgive him. It took me a long time to make her say: 'I forgive my son.' Just before she died in my arms, she was able to say that with a real forgiveness. She was not concerned that she was dying. The breaking of the heart was that her son did not want her. This is something you and I can understand."[13]

Do you see Mother Teresa's compassion for this woman shining through her words? She knew that peace would come to this heart-broken mother only as she learned to forgive the one who had wronged her—her own son.

Forgiveness is an important part of compassion, for it is only as we are able to empathize with and understand the person who has wronged us that we will be able to forgive them and find peace for ourselves.

Paul writes, *"And become useful and helpful and kind to one another, tenderhearted (compassionate, understanding, loving-hearted), forgiving one another [readily and freely], as God in Christ forgave you"* (Eph. 4:32). This is compassion's lifestyle, the qualities that are desperately needed in society today.

Mother Teresa expressed her feelings about life and her relationship with Jesus Christ in the following poem:

He is the Life that I want to live,

He is the Light that I want to radiate.

He is the Way to the Father.

He is the Love with which I want to love.

He is the Joy that I want to share.

He is the Peace that I want to sow.

Jesus is everything to me.

Without Him, I can do nothing. [14]

SOMETHING BEAUTIFUL FOR GOD

In 1969, Malcolm Muggeridge produced a documentary about Mother Teresa's life. It was entitled, "Something Beautiful for God." In 1971, he wrote a book with the same title.

These two works helped to spread the name of Mother Teresa around the world. She became the best known missionary in the world and people everywhere respected her life and her work.

She received many accolades and awards, including the first Pope John XXIII Peace Prize (1971), the Kennedy Prize (1971), the Balzan Prize for humanity, peace, and brotherhood among peoples (1978), the Albert Schweitzer International Prize (1975), the United States Presidential Medal of Freedom (1985), the Congressional Gold Medal (1994), honorary citizenship of the United States (1996), the Nobel Peace Prize (1997), and honorary degrees from numerous colleges and universities.

Hers was a life well-lived, and she became "something beautiful for God," indeed. In 1999 a Gallup poll found that Mother Teresa was "the most admired person of the 20th century."

In 1982, Mother Teresa was successful in persuading the Israelis and Palestinians to stop shooting long enough to enable her organization to rescue 37 retarded children from a hospital in Beirut. The love and compassion she exhibited is needed in the Middle East today.

In the 1980s and '90s her health began to decline. She suffered her first heart attack in 1983 while she was visiting Pope John Paul II in

Rome. She received a pacemaker after her second heart attack in 1989. Then, when she was in Mexico in 1991, she developed pneumonia, which led to further heart problems.

In the face of her deteriorating health, Mother Teresa offered to resign as the head of the Missionaries of Charity, but the sisters had a vote, and all of them voted for her to remain in leadership, so she continued on with her ministry.

In April 1996, Mother Teresa suffered a fall that caused her to break her collar bone. In August of that same year she suffered from malaria, and the left ventricle of her heart failed, causing her to undergo heart surgery.

On March 13, 1997, she stepped down as the head of her order and she died later that year, on September 5, 1997. She was 87 years old.

At the time of her death there were more than 4,000 sisters who served with the Missionaries of Charity around the world. In addition, 300 brothers became associated with the order along with over 100,000 lay volunteers. These devoted servants of God operated 610 missions in 123 countries, including hospices, homes for people with HIV/AIDS, leprosy and tuberculosis sanitariums, soup kitchens, children and family counseling programs, orphanages, and schools.

This humble woman who came from a poor, obscure village in Macedonia, rose to become the most respected woman in the world, because she was faithful to the call God gave to her. She devoted her life to serving others. She became a role model of compassion for all of us to follow.

PEACE AND JOY

Mother Teresa has often been compared to Saint Francis of Assisi, the 13th-century friar who found his joy in serving others. She loved his lifestyle of compassion, poverty, and service, and she learned a great deal from him.

She was fond of praying (and living) St. Francis' well-known prayer:

Lord, make me an instrument of your peace;

Where there is hatred, let me sow love;

Where there is injury, pardon;

Where there is despair, hope.

O Divine Master, grant that I might seek

Not so much to be consoled, as to console;

To be understood, as to understand;

Not so much to be loved, as to love another.

For it is in giving that we receive;

It is in pardoning that we are pardoned;

It is in dying that we are born to eternal life.

Mother Teresa was an instrument of peace in the world. The former Secretary-General of the United Nations, Javier Perez de Cuellar, said about her: "She is the United Nations. She is peace in the world."

"DO SMALL THINGS WITH GREAT LOVE."

One of Mother Teresa's best-known mottos: "Do small things with great love." This simple, but profound advice is what the world needs today. She also said, "Never forget you are co-workers of Jesus."

These two quotations form the framework of Mother Teresa's life and ministry, and, when we apply them to our own lives, we will see exciting changes taking place in our life and ministry.

Let her prayer become your prayer, as you contemplate the call to compassion in your own life:

Lead me from death to life, from falsehood to truth;

Lead me from despair to hope, from fear to trust.

Lead me from hate to love, from war to peace.

Let peace fill our hearts, our world, our universe.

Peace. Peace. Peace. [15]

Let the peace and compassion of Jesus fill your heart. Follow the trail that Mother Teresa has blazed, and walk in the footsteps of Jesus: *"For even to this were you called [it is inseparable from your vocation]. For*

Christ also suffered for you, leaving you [His personal] example, so that you should follow in His footsteps" (1 Pet. 2:21).

In conclusion, I offer a simple quote from Mother Teresa that seems to reveal the secret of her success in service to others. I ask you to reflect on her words and apply them to your life: "When there is a call within a call, there is only one thing to do, to say 'yes' to Jesus. That's all. If we belong to him, he must be able to use us without consulting us.... I had only to say a simple 'yes.'"[16]

Dear Heavenly Father, In Jesus name we come before you to offer our lives to help your children—young and old—in whatever way is right and lovely in your eyes. May we follow the example of Jesus when He ministered to them out of love and compassion. Your example is the only example we need; your love is the only love we need to share with others—for it is pure and holy and nourishment to body and spirit. In the precious name of Jesus, Amen.

ENDNOTES

1. Eileen Egan and Kathleen Egan, OSB, eds., *Suffering Into Joy*, (Ann Arbor, MI: Servant Publications, 1994), 21.

2. http://www.cnn.com, 2006.

3. Egan and Egan, *Suffering Into Joy*, 13.

4. http://nobelprize.org.

5. http://en.wikipedia.org.

6. John Paul II, Address of John Paul II to the Pilgrims Who Had Come to Rome for the Beatification of Mother Teresa, 2003.

7. Benedict XVI, *Deus Caritas Est.*

8. Egan and Egan, *Suffering Into Joy*, 14.

9. Egan and Egan, *Suffering Into Joy*, 22.

10. Egan and Egan, *Suffering Into Joy*, 32-33.

11. http://nobelprize.org/peace/laureates/1979/teresa-lecture.html.

12. http://priestsforlife.org/brochures/mtspeech.html.

13. http://en.wikipedia.org.

14. http://home.comcast.net/~motherteresasite/autobiog.html.

15. Egan and Egan, *Suffering Into Joy*, 140-141.

16. Egan and Egan, *Suffering Into Joy*, 65.

chapter eight

Little Women—Big God
by
Michal Ann Goll

*So let us open our hearts wide to love. Love is the mightiest thing
in the world. Love makes us to love and to do. God is Love. I can
do all things through Love which strengtheneth me.*[1]

Amy Carmichael, 1867-1951

This chapter focuses on the lives and ministries of five little ladies
who became great women of God: Amy Carmichael, Catherine Drexel,
Phoebe Palmer, Hannah More, and Elizabeth Fry. Each one of their
hearts was filled with compassion, and they spent their lives in service to
God by helping others.

As I have studied their lives and writings, I have been deeply
stirred to become more like them, for these women lived close to God
and they shared His life with the people He brought to them. I'm sure
you will be impressed, as I was, by their uncompromising devotion to
the Lord.

God called each of these ladies to acts of compassion and uncommon valor. They were women after God's own heart, ladies of character
who lived their lives in sold-out commitment to the Father. As you read
their stories, may you respond to His call, as well, for He is looking for

those who will obey Him by going forth into the whitened harvest fields during these last days of human history.

ABANDONED TO GOD—AMY CARMICHAEL

Amy Carmichael was born on December 16, 1867, in Millisle, a small village in Northern Ireland. As its name implies, this was a place of mills, flour mills to be precise, and this was the type of business which enabled Amy's father to acquire considerable wealth.

Unfortunately, however, her father died when Amy was 18 years old, and this resulted in financial uncertainty for the Carmichael family, which was subsequently forced to move to Belfast.

Amy was the oldest of seven children. One wintry Sunday morning, as the family was returning home from the Presbyterian church they attended, Amy and her two brothers saw an old woman who was carrying a large bundle. All the children wanted to help her, but they felt somewhat embarrassed about asking her if they could help. Nonetheless, they went to her aid.

Amy writes, "This meant facing all the respectable people who were, like ourselves, on their way home. It was a horrid moment. We were only two boys and a girl, and not at all exalted Christians. We hated doing it. Crimson all over (at least we felt crimson, soul and body of us) we plodded on, a wet wind blows in about us, and blowing, too, the rags of that poor old woman, till she seemed like a bundle of feathers and we unhappily mixed up with them."[2]

As they kept walking, they came to a beautiful Victorian fountain. Just as they were passing this fountain, Amy heard a voice that was speaking the words of a Scripture verse: *"Now if any man build upon this foundation gold, silver, precious stones, wood, hay, stubble; every man's work shall be made manifest; for the day shall declare it, because it shall be revealed by fire; and the fire shall try every man's work of what sort it is. If any man's work abide..."* (1 Cor. 3:12-14 KJV).

Startled by this message, Amy turned around to see who had spoken it to her, but no one was there, and all she heard then was the bubbling and splashing of the fountain and a few distant passersby who were talking with each other.[3]

She knew then that God was calling her to "settle some things with Him."[3] Prior to this she had been primarily preoccupied with her social life.

The death of her father caused Amy to reevaluate her values and beliefs, and she began to think seriously about her future and God's plan for her life. As a result, she began to work in an inner-city mission in Belfast.

THE HIGHER CHRISTIAN LIFE

The Carmichaels traveled to Cumbria County, England, in order to attend a Keswick Conference in England's Lake District. The convention had begun a decade or so earlier as an important gathering of evangelical Christians. It was the center of what came to be known as the Higher Life Movement in Great Britain. Personal holiness was the major emphasis of this movement.[4]

Amy Carmichael was greatly influenced by her experience there. She writes, "The hall was full of a sort of gray mist, very dull and chilly. I came to that meeting half hoping, half fearing. Would there be anything for me? ...the fog in the Hall seemed to soak into me. My soul was in a fog. Then the chairman rose for the last prayer...'O Lord, we know Thou art able to keep us from falling.' Those words found me. It was as if they were alight. And they shone for me."[5]

This was the moment when Amy Carmichael realized that she must dedicate her whole life to the Lord Jesus Christ, who had given His life for her. In her heart of hearts she understood that she had to do the same in return and give her all to Him.

Amy began to realize that she had to die to the self-life in order to follow the Lord's leading. She knew the meaning of Paul's words, *"I have been crucified with Christ [in Him I have shared His crucifixion]; it is no longer I who live, but Christ (the Messiah) lives in me; and the life I now live in the body I live by faith in (by adherence to and reliance on and complete trust in) the Son of God, Who loved me and gave Himself up for me"* (Gal. 2:20).

Nothing but complete surrender to Jesus could satisfy her now, and she determined to give her life in total abandonment to Him. It is imperative for each of us to do the same. We must surrender all to Jesus so that He can live His life through us and we can be His hands extended, reaching out to the oppressed.

In 1887, Amy heard China Inland Mission founder, Hudson Taylor, speak, and his compelling message ignited her passion for missions. In 1893, she left for Japan with the support of the Keswick Convention, but this initial introduction to foreign missionary service was a big disappointment to her, because she felt there was little difference between the missionaries she worked with there and people in the world.

She wrote, "… we are here just what we are at home—not one bit better—and the devil is awfully busy…There are missionary shipwrecks of once fair vessels."[6] Amy wanted more of God, and her desire to live a holy life before Him pushed her away from her work in Japan. She decided to return home, but on her way back to England, she stopped in Ceylon to help care for a sick family friend.

Upon returning home, she continued seeking God and His will for her life. After less than a year back home, she decided to return to the mission field. This time she went to India—the place God had picked for her. It was 1895 and she was commissioned by the Church of England Zenana Missionary Society to go to Dohnavur, India, where she served for 56 years without a furlough!

GOD'S DEVOTED SERVANT—"AMMA"

Amy Carmichael founded the Dohnavur Fellowship for Girls, which was a ministry that was devoted to rescuing girls whose families had dedicated them to become temple prostitutes.

Through her ministry more than 1,000 children were rescued from abuse and neglect. The children called her "Amma," which means "mother" in the Tamil language, and Amy truly became a mother to them.

She wrote, "There were days when the sky turned black for me because of what I heard and knew was true…. Sometimes it was as if I saw the Lord Jesus Christ kneeling alone, as He knelt long ago under the olive trees…. And the only thing that one who cared could do was to go softly and kneel down beside Him, so that He would not be alone in His sorrow over the little children."[7]

Amy Carmichael was a devout woman of prayer, and her life was characterized by total commitment, all-out compassion, obedience, and selflessness. One of her most heart-felt prayers, a prayer that became the theme of her life, was expressed in the following poem:

O Father, help, lest our poor love refuse

For our beloved the life that they would choose,

And in our fear of loss for them, or pain,

Forget eternal gain.

Show us the gain, the golden harvest there

For corn of wheat that they have buried here;

Lest human love defraud them and betray,

Teach us, O God, to pray.

Teach us to pray, remembering Calvary,

For as the Master must the servant be;

We see their face set toward Jerusalem,

Let us not hinder them.

Teach us to pray; O Thou who didst not spare

Thine own Beloved, lead us on in prayer;

Purge from the earthly, give us love Divine,

Father, like Thine, like Thine.[8]

Amy Carmichael wrote 35 books, many of which continue to inspire people around the world today. She was crippled by a fall in 1931, and four years later she became bedridden. She remained an invalid thereafter and died on January 18, 1851, and was buried in her beloved Dohnavur.

For more than 50 years Amy's overarching goal in life was: "To save children in moral danger; to train them to serve others; to succor the desolate and the suffering; to do anything that may be shown to be the will of our heavenly Father, in order to make His love known, especially to the people of India."

THE "MILLIONAIRE NUN"— CATHERINE DREXEL

Catherine Mary Drexel was born in Philadelphia, Pennsylvania, in 1858. She was the second daughter of a wealthy Philadelphia banker—Francis Martin Drexel and his wife, Hannah Langstroth. Her mother died approximately one month after Catherine was born.

Catherine's sister, Elizabeth, was three years older than she was. When her father remarried, another sister, Louise, was born in 1863. Francis's new wife, Emma Bouvier, became a very devoted mother to Catherine and her sisters.

The Drexel girls did not go to school; they were "home schooled" by governesses. Nonetheless, Catherine was well-educated and her natural intelligence became obvious to all when she was very young.

As she grew up, she was able to travel extensively with her family and this broadened Catherine's understanding of the world and its people. On one trip to the Southwest, Catherine saw firsthand the deprivation of native Indian-Americans and she was appalled to see the deplorable conditions in which they lived.

This caused her to resolve to do something to help the poor when she got older and this may well have been the time when her heart for missions began to develop. Around this same time, she also began to become deeply concerned about the plight of African Americans.

Catherine's parents instilled in their children the concept that wealth was a gift from God that He wanted them to share with others.[9]

SHARING THE WEALTH

Jesus said, "Cure the sick, raise the dead, cleanse the lepers, drive out demons. Freely (without pay) you have received, freely (without charge) give" (Matt. 10:8). This was Catherine Drexel's approach to life and ministry when she became a nun in 1889.

She entered the Sisters of Mercy convent in Pittsburgh, Pennsylvania, where she prepared for her vows. While there, she began to sense that God was calling her to a ministry to the poor.

Later that same year, Catherine took her first vows of poverty, chastity, and obedience—vows to which she was faithful throughout her life of compassionate service to God and His people.

Catherine had a personal visit with Pope Leo XIII in 1883. She asked him what could be done for the Indians and blacks in the United States. The pope answered, "Daughter, why don't you become a missionary?" His question stirred something deep inside her; she felt she had heard God's challenge, and she began to weep.[10]

Clearly, God was calling Catherine to missionary service; and as a result, she began to envision a new order of nuns who would serve Native Americans and African Americans in particular. When she returned to America, she consulted with her spiritual director, Bishop James O'Conner. He advised her to start her own religious community.

SISTERS OF THE BLESSED SACRAMENT

The new order—the Sisters of the Blessed Sacrament for Indians and Colored People—was founded on February 12, 1891; and Catherine Drexel took the name of Mother Katharine Drexel. Because she was a multimillionaire and had taken the vow of poverty, Archbishop Patrick Ryan of Philadelphia reminded her that she needed to be willing to surrender her funds to the Lord's work.

From then on, she lived a very austere life, using money for herself only to provide for the basic necessities of life. Though she was rich, she voluntarily became a poor woman who ministered to the poor, and she realized that everything she had belonged to God. This reminds me of a Scripture about Jesus:

For you are becoming progressively acquainted with and recognizing more strongly and clearly the grace of our Lord Jesus Christ (His kindness, His gracious generosity, His undeserved favor and spiritual blessing), [in] that though he was [so very] rich, yet for your sakes He became [so very] poor, in order that by

His poverty you might become enriched (abundantly supplied)
(2 Corinthians 8:9).

Mother Katharine began to use her money for God. She started by building a convent in Bensalem, Pennsylvania, not far from her native Philadelphia. In her lifetime she freely gave nearly $20 million from her parents' estate to the poor. She established 60 missions to provide education for Indians and blacks, and she and her sisters dedicated their lives completely to the welfare of these disadvantaged people.[11]

Along the way, Mother Katharine and her sisters encountered great opposition, particularly from people with racial prejudices. She never wavered in the face of conflict, however, and eventually won the respect of many people, even of former enemies. She always stood stalwartly for justice, mercy, and peace.

Katharine was a woman who believed in the power of prayer. She asked God to intervene in the lives of Native Americans and African Americans and to stem the tide of racism in the United States. Though the Civil War had ended a few decades earlier, she realized that many blacks were still not free and had to live in substandard conditions as sharecroppers and menial laborers.

She recognized that Indians and blacks were denied the rights of full citizenship and equality in many places and that those who were able to attend school received poor educations. As a result, she developed "a compassionate urgency to help change racial attitudes in the United States."[12]

In 1915, Mother Katharine was responsible for the establishment of Xavier University in New Orleans, which was then the only Catholic university for blacks in America.

Throughout her long and devoted life, Catherine Drexel held true to the stated goals of the order she founded:

1. The primary object which the Sisters of this religious con gregation purpose to themselves is their own personal sanctification.

2. The secondary and special object of the members of the congregation is to apply themselves zealously to the service of Our Lord...by endeavoring to lead the Indian and

Colored races to the knowledge and love of God, and so make them living temples of our Lord's divinity.[13]

A TRUE SAINT

The Roman Catholic Church canonized Mother Katharine Drexel in 2000. In her lifetime of service to God and His Church she accomplished:

- The founding of 49 convents for her sisters.
- The establishment of training courses for teachers.
- The building of 62 schools, including Xavier University.
- Numerous writings.
- Helping to change the attitudes of church people toward the poor and disenfranchised.
- A life of holiness, prayer, and total giving of herself.
- An example of courage, mercy, justice, and compassion.

The Vatican news service described her life as follows: "In her quiet way, Katharine combined prayerful and total dependence on Divine Providence with determined activism. Her joyous incisiveness attuned to the Holy Spirit, penetrated obstacles and facilitated her advances for social justice. Through the prophetic witness of Katharine Drexel's initiative, the Church in the United States was enabled to become aware of the grave domestic need for an apostolate among Native Americans and Afro-Americans. She did not hesitate to speak out against injustice, taking a public stance when racial discrimination was in evidence."[14]

Catherine Drexel died on March 3, 1955, after living for Jesus and walking in compassion for almost a century.

THE MOTHER OF THE HOLINESS MOVEMENT—PHOEBE PALMER

Phoebe (nee Worrall) Palmer was born in New York City on December 17, 1807. Her father, Henry Worrall, was a devout Methodist, who had experienced a radical conversion during the Wesleyan Revival in England before he immigrated to America. He married an American, Dorothea Wade.

Phoebe's parents made sure that they had family worship twice a day in their home. They placed high value on "religious conversion and holy living" for themselves and their children.[15] When she was only 11 years old, Phoebe wrote this poem on the flyleaf of her Bible:

This revelation—holy, just, and true

Though oft I read, it seems forever new;

While light from heaven upon its pages rest,

I feel its power, and with it I am blessed.

Henceforth, I take thee as my future guide,

Let naught from thee my youthful heart divide.

And then, if late or early death be mine,

All will be well, since I, O Lord, am Thine![15]

Throughout her life Phoebe kept the Bible as her guidebook, and the power of the Word motivated her to spread the concept of holiness throughout America in great love and compassion for everyone she met.

TRAGEDY AND PERSEVERANCE

Phoebe married a homeopathic physician in 1827. His name was Walter Clarke Palmer, and he, like Phoebe, was an active member of the Methodist Episcopal Church. His parents, Miles and Deborah Clarke Palmer, had helped to establish the denomination in New York City.

The young couple shared a commitment to Christ and each other, but their marriage and faith were severely tested by a series of hardships and tragedies, including the deaths of three of their children. At first, Phoebe felt that the deaths of her children were evidence of God's displeasure with her, and she began to question her salvation as she struggled with despair, guilt, and remorse.

This thrust her into a deeper pursuit of God and His ways. After the death of her second son, she wrote, "I will not attempt to describe the pressure of the last crushing trial. Surely I needed it, or it would not have been given. God takes our treasure to heaven, that our hearts may be there also. The Lord had declared himself a jealous God, he will have no other gods before him. After my loved ones were snatched away, I saw that I had concentrated my time and attentions far too exclusively, to the neglect of the religious activities demanded. Though painfully learned, yet I trust the lesson has been fully apprehended. From henceforth, Jesus must and shall have the uppermost seat in my heart."[16]

"DEEPER WORK OF GRACE"

Phoebe's sister, Sarah Lankford, began having weekly prayer meetings with Methodist women. Within two years or so Phoebe assumed leadership of these meetings, which became known as "the Tuesday Meeting for the Promotion of Holiness." Eventually men began to attend these gatherings, as well.

As word of these meetings spread around the country, a great interest began to develop in what became known as the Holiness Movement.

Phoebe and her husband became itinerant preachers, and they received invitations to speak on holiness—the "deeper work of grace" from churches, conferences, and camp meetings. Phoebe's work encouraged many other women to start meetings for the promotion of holiness throughout America.

In the autumn of 1857 the Palmers went to Hamilton, Ontario, Canada, to speak at an afternoon prayer meeting. This prayer meeting turned into a ten-day revival in which hundreds of people chose Christ as their Savior.

When they returned to New York, they preached to standing-room-only crowds, and then they traveled to England, where many found faith in Christ. They remained in England for a few years, and it is estimated that more than 25,000 people came to the knowledge of Christ through Phoebe's ministry.

The Palmers believed in a deeper work of grace which would lead to holiness, and this concept was based on John Wesley's idea of Christian perfection, a belief that a Christian can live a life free of serious sin. This "deeper work of grace" was what the Palmers called "entire sanctification."[17]

THE WAY OF HOLINESS

Without any question, Phoebe Palmer played a prominent role in spreading the concept of Christian holiness throughout America and around the world. She wrote several books on this topic, including *The Way of Holiness*—a foundational book in the Holiness Movement.

She was very influential in the lives of several women, including Frances Willard, a leading advocate in the Temperance Movement and Catherine Booth, the cofounder of the Salvation Army.

In her book, *The Promise of the Father*, Phoebe Palmer took a strong stand in behalf of the role of women in Christian ministry. She based this on Acts 5:29, which urges us to obey God rather than men. She said, "It is always right to obey the Holy Spirit's command, and if that is laid upon a woman to preach the Gospel, then it is right for her to do so; it is a duty she cannot neglect without falling into condemnation."[18] Her teaching opened the door for many women preachers to respond to God's call in their lives.

Mrs. Palmer's holiness was reflected in every aspect of her life, and it impelled her to help found the Five Points Mission in a slum area of New York City in 1850. She also served as a leader in the Methodist Ladies' Home Missionary Society. Her faith had "legs," as it moved in compassion among the dregs of society.

Other influential books by Phoebe Palmer include *Entire Devotion to God* and *Faith and Its Effects*, both of which were published in the 1840s.

When her daughter, Eliza, was burned to death as the result of a fire in her nursery, Phoebe wrote these words that prophetically described what her life and ministry truly became: "While pacing the room, crying to God, amid the tumult of grief, my mind was arrested by a gentle whisper, saying, 'Your Heavenly Father loves you. He would not permit such a great trial, without intending that some great good proportionate in magnitude and weight should result. He means to teach you some great lesson that might not otherwise be learned.'...My darling is in heaven doing an angel service. And now I have resolved, that the service, or in other words, the time I would have devoted to her, shall be spent in work for Jesus. And if diligent and self-sacrificing in carrying out my resolve, the death of this child may result in the spiritual life of many...."[19]

Phoebe Palmer held true to this commitment until her death on November 2, 1874, and as a result, thousands came to know Christ personally, walking in holiness throughout their lives.

CHAMPION OF THE DISENFRANCHISED— HANNAH MORE

Hannah More, like Amy Carmichael, Catherine Drexel, and Phoebe Palmer, was a woman who loved God with all her heart, mind, and soul, and loved other people as herself. (See Matthew 22:37-39.)

She was born at Stapleton, near Bristol, England, in 1745, the youngest of the five daughters of Jacob More, who had been a Presbyterian, but became a member of the Church of England. Jacob was a teacher, and his older daughters followed in his footsteps by founding a boarding school at Bristol. Hannah became a pupil in her sisters' school when she was 12 years old. Eventually she became a teacher there, as well.

Hannah began writing for publication when she was still a teenager. Her early works were mostly pastoral plays, which were written for young ladies.

She became engaged to William Turner, a wealthy squire, who was 20 years older than her. The couple never married, but William provided Hannah with an annuity that enabled her to become financially independent.

By the mid-1790s, Hannah became closely involved with the Clapham Sect of evangelical Christians, a group that became very involved in the abolitionist movement. The well-known anti-slavery advocate William Wilberforce and the former slave captain, John Newton, attended these meetings, as well.

ABOLITION OF THE SLAVE TRADE

Hannah More was the most influential female member of the Society for the Effecting the Abolition of the African Slave Trade. She wrote a number of religious tracts that eventually led to the formation of the Religious Tracts Society. Several of her tracts opposed slavery and the slave trade.

She became friends with Wilberforce and other anti-slavery leaders, including John Newton, who wrote "Amazing Grace;" and in 1788 she published a poem entitled "Slavery." In the late 1780s Hannah and her sister, Martha More, conducted philanthropic work in the Mendip area, a poor coal-mining region. They set up 12 schools by 1800, and in these schools, reading, the Bible, and Christian teaching were central. They encountered considerable opposition along the way, because many farmers felt that education would become fatal to agriculture.[20] At the same time, the Anglican clergy of the area accused Hannah of having "Methodist tendencies."[21]

Clearly, Hannah "blazed a trail" for women in her day. She believed in justice for all people. She was a pioneer in the abolitionist movement, which eventually brought an end to slavery in Great Britain and the United States. She chose to get involved in the world instead of living a life of quiet obscurity, which she could have chosen because she became quite wealthy as a result of the publication of her numerous books, plays, poems, and tracts.

In fact, she developed a "cottage industry" that enabled her to print millions of religious tracts, which were distributed around the world.

In the life of Hannah More we see a woman who was yielded to God—a great "…example of balance: the hearts of Mary and Martha beating within the same bosom. Hannah More proves that you can be passionate about His presence and at the same time be a servant to fellow man. She earned credibility in two realms, so that both worlds would heed her invitations. If you build it *He* will come…and *they* will come to see Him."[22]

Hannah More was also instrumental in the establishment of Sunday schools in the Wrington, England, area; and in these schools poor children were taught reading, religion, and personal hygiene.

AN INFLUENTIAL WRITER AND A WOMAN OF PRAYER

Hannah More was a prolific writer of dramas, poetry, and prose. Many of her works were spiritually and ethically influential in the lives of women: *Strictures on Female Education* (1799), *Character of a Young Princess* (1805), *Practical Piety* (1811), *Christian Morals* (1813), *Character of St. Paul* (1815), *and Moral Sketches* (1819).

Even though most of her writings have been forgotten now, her works were extremely popular and highly marketable during her day, and they had a great impact on women throughout the English-speaking world.

Hannah More wrote, "Prayer is not eloquence, but earnestness; not the definition of helplessness, but the feeling of it; not figures of speech, but earnestness of soul."[23]

When she died in 1833, Hannah More left the equivalent of $3 million to charities and religious societies. She is buried in the graveyard of All Saints' Church in Wrington.

I conclude this section by quoting from one of Hannah's poems in which she writes about her heavenly home, where she now resides:

The soul on earth is an immortal guest,

Compelled to starve at an unreal feast;

A pilgrim panting for the rest to come;

An exile, anxious for his native home.[24]

PRISON REFORMER—ELIZABETH FRY

Elizabeth (nee Gurney) Fry was born in Norwich, England, on May 21, 1780. Her father was John Gurney, a successful businessman who was a member of the Society of Friends (Quakers). He was a partner in the Gurney Bank and the owner of a wool-stapling and spinning factory. Elizabeth's mother, Catherine Gurney, was a member of the Society of Friends, as well, and she was extensively involved in charity work among the poor. Catherine required her children to spend two hours a day in quiet worship of the Lord.

Elizabeth was 12 when her mother died soon after the birth of her twelfth child. As one of the older daughters, she was required to help in the raising of her younger siblings. Assuming the responsibilities of an adult and a parent caused Elizabeth to grow up fairly quickly.

REFRESHING SHOWERS
ON PARCHED UP EARTH

She became familiar with the writings of Mary Wollstonecraft, who wrote *Vindication of the Rights of Women,* and she studied the writings of the abolitionists of her day. At this point in her life, Elizabeth seemed to be heading in a liberal, non-religious direction.

When she was 18 years old, however, Elizabeth heard an American Quaker named William Savery, preach in Norwich. She was so impressed by what Savery had to say that she begged her father to invite the preacher to dinner. Her father did so, and after her meeting with Savery, Elizabeth wrote these words: "Today I felt there is a God. I loved the man as if he was almost sent from heaven—we had much serious talk and what he said to me was like a refreshing shower on parched up earth."[25]

This was a dramatic turning point in Elizabeth's life. She wrote, "After we had spent a pleasant evening, my heart began to feel itself silenced before God and without looking at others, I felt myself under the shadow of the wing of God.... After the meeting my heart felt really light and as I walked home by starlight, I looked through nature up to nature's God"[26]

The "showers" from Heaven that Elizabeth experienced that night caused her to make a momentous decision in her life. From then on she determined to devote her energies to helping needy people. She began to collect used clothing for the poor, she visited the sick, and she opened up a Sunday school in her home where she taught poor children to read.

She wrote, "Since my heart was touched...I believe I never have awakened from sleep, in sickness or in health, by day or by night, without my first waking thought being, 'how best I might serve my Lord.'"[27] Clearly, her conversion to Christ went deep, and its repercussions were felt around the world.

Soon thereafter she was appointed to the committee that was responsible for running the Society of Friends' school at Acworth.

A NEW MINISTRY

In the summer of 1799, Elizabeth met Joseph Fry, a Quaker who was the son of a prosperous merchant in Essex. They were married in the summer of the following year. God blessed this young couple with eight children.

In March 1811, Elizabeth became a preacher for the Society of Friends. A friend, Stephen Grellet, told Elizabeth about the horrific conditions that existed at Newgate Prison, which he had recently visited. He was particularly shocked by the way the women who were incarcerated there were being treated.

They had to sleep on the floor without nightclothes or any kind of bedding, and 300 women were huddled together in only two wards. These prisoners had to cook, wash, and sleep in the same cell.

After hearing this upsetting description, Elizabeth decided to visit the women of Newgate Prison herself, and she did so on a regular basis thereafter. She took clothing to them and started a school and chapel in the prison. As time went on, she established a new system of administration there, as well, and this included matrons and monitors who supervised the women.

Meanwhile, Elizabeth continued her duties as a wife and mother, and three more children were born to the Frys. During this period Elizabeth had to endure the grief and mourning associated with the loss of her 5-year-old daughter, Betsy.

Elizabeth and 11 other Quakers founded the Association for the Improvement of the Female Prisoners in Newgate. In her address to the House of Commons, Elizabeth described the conditions of the women in Newgate Prison: "...each with a space of about six feet by two to herself...old and young, hardened offenders with those who had committed only a minor offence or their first crime; the lowest of women with the respectable married women and maid-servants."[28]

Her work influenced major changes in the penal system in Great Britain, which housed all sorts of criminals and punished them with tortures that were arbitrary at best. Richard Huntsman writes, "For misdemeanours such as causing a nuisance, the culprit would expect physical punishments such as being whipped, branded or put in the stocks.

"For minor offences, such as stealing a teaspoon or merely begging, one could, before 1775, expect transportation to North America for 7 or 14 years to serve as an indentured labourer or servant. During that period some 40,000 men and women were transported to North America and the West Indies.

"For what were seen as serious offences ranging from murder, forgery or stealing any object worth over 5 shillings (a week's wage for a maid 'living in'), one would expect to be hanged. Hence the advice that you might as well be hanged for stealing a sheep as a lamb! In all, over 300 offences attracted the death penalty."[29]

It was these unjust penalties and unfair conditions that caused Elizabeth Fry to get fully involved in prison reform. When she would visit the women at Newgate, she would often read the Bible to them.

Between 1818 and 1843, Elizabeth visited prisons throughout the British Isles and the continent of Europe. It was an exhausting and dangerous journey. She would seek the approval of local officials before entering the prisons, and after her visits, she would organize a ladies' association to continue her work in each local prison.

She also became involved as an advocate for ladies who were sentenced to death. Often she was able to save them from being hanged.

Her constant prayer was, "O Lord, may I be directed what to do and what to leave undone."[30]

AN EXPANDING OUTREACH

In 1824, Elizabeth visited Brighton and was shocked by the number of beggars and poor people she encountered there. This led her to form the Brighton District Visiting Society, a group of women who would visit in the homes of the poor and provide them with physical, emotional, and spiritual help and comfort.

She campaigned for the homeless in London and tried to improve the care that was given to mental patients in the asylums throughout England. She also worked arduously for the reform of workhouses and hospitals throughout her country.

Nursing care became another concern of Elizabeth's. She established a training school for nurses in 1840. Florence Nightingale once wrote to Elizabeth to let her know what a great influence she had been in her life. In 1840, Fry founded the Protestant Sisters of Charity, an organization of nurses who made themselves available to families in need.

Elizabeth often met with Queen Victoria, and the monarch contributed money to her ministry. The queen wrote that she considered Elizabeth Fry to be a "very superior person."[31]

In 1827, Fry published a book, *Observations, on the Visiting Superintendence and Government of Female Prisoners*, in which she showed the need for prison reform and called for greater opportunities for women. She also condemned the death penalty.

After a short illness, Elizabeth Fry died on October 12, 1845. Over a thousand mourners stood in silence as she was buried at the Society of Friends graveyard at Barking.

She was a woman of eminent compassion and strong faith, who surely believed these words of Paul: *"The only thing that counts is faith expressing itself through love"* (Gal. 5:6 NIV).

Dear Father in Heaven, As the saints who have lived before us, may we find those who need your touch of compassion and may we share with them the goodness of your love. May we find the lost, feed the hungry, speak for the voiceless, and provide shelter for the homeless. Please give us the courage we need to seek out those in the greatest need. In Jesus' name, Amen.

ENDNOTES

1. Amy Carmichael, *Thou Givest…They Gather* (Fort Washington, PA: Christian Literature Crusade, Donhavur Fellowship, 1958), 134.

2. http://www.intouch.org/myintouch/mighty/portraits/amy_carmichael_213673.htm.

3. Ibid.

4. http://en.wikipedia.org/wiki/Keswick_Convention.

5. http://www.intouch.org/myintouch/mighty/portraits/amy_carmichael_213673.htm.

6. http://www.traveltheroad.com/missions/missionaries/carmichael.php.

7. http://www.intouch.org/myintouch/mighty/portraits/amy_carmichael_213673.htm.

8. Amy Carmichael, *Thou Givest…They Gather*, 134.

9. http://www.ewtn.com/library/mary/drexel.htm.

10. http://www.allformary.org/AmericanSaints/drexel.htm.

11. Ibid.

12. http://www.vatican.va/news_services/liturgy/saints/ns_lit_doc_2001001katharine_drexel.

13. http://www.allformary.org/AmericanSaints/drexel.htm.

14. http://are.as.wvu.edu/phebe.htm.

15. Rev. Richard Wheatley, *The Life and Letters of Mrs. Phoebe Palmer.* (New York: Palmer and Hughes, 1876), 18.

16. Ibid., 26.

17. http://en.wikipedia.org/wiki/Phoebe_Palmer.

18. http://are.as.wvu.edu/phebe.htm.

19. Ibid.

20. http://en.wikipedia.org/wiki/Hannah_More.

21. http://en.wikipedia.org/wiki/Hannah_More.

22. Tommy Tenney, *Mary's Prayers and Martha's Recipes* (Shippensburg, PA: Fresh Bread, 2002), 18.

23. *Women's Wisdom Through the Ages*, (New York, NY: Testament Books, 1994), 56.

24. Ibid., 39.

25. http://www.spartacus.schoolnet.co.uk/REFry.htm.

26. *Women's Wisdom Through the Ages*, 5.

27. Ibid., 23.

28. http://www.spartacus.schoonet.co.uk/REFry.htm.

29. Richard Huntsman, *Elizabeth Fry: Quaker and Prison Reformer* (Guist Bottom, Dereham, Norfolk, UK: Larks Press, 1998), 3.

30. *Women's Wisdom Through the Ages*, 127.

31. http://www.spartacus.schoolnet.co.uk/REFry.htm.

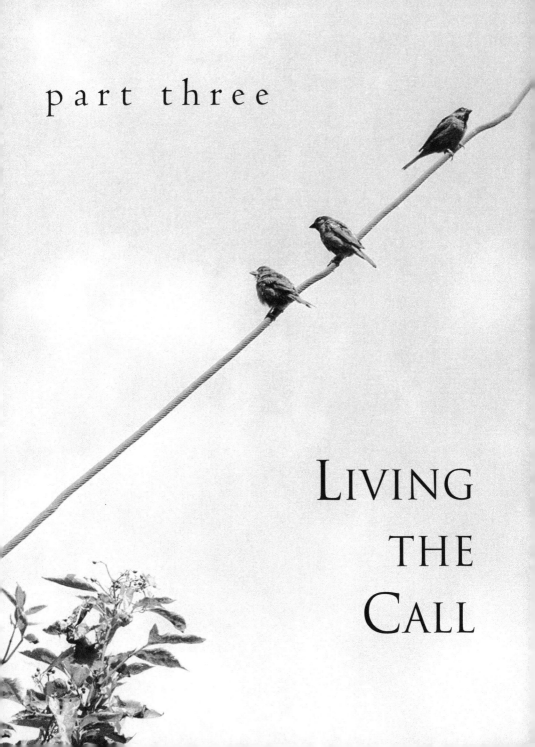

part three

LIVING
THE
CALL

This final part of our book is a call to compassion and action toward the horrific condition of the poor in our world. You will be stunned to discover the extent of poverty and the suffering it is bringing to millions. We hope that you are so stunned that you will be moved to take action on their behalf. This widespread social phenomenon has resulted in poverty of spirit, disease, death, depression, hunger, homelessness, and many other maladies.

The Bible says, *"Do justice to the weak (poor) and fatherless; maintain the rights of the afflicted and needy. Deliver the poor and needy; rescue them out of the hand of the wicked"* (Ps. 82:3-4). This is what the women portrayed in Part II did, and it is what you and I must do as well. You can be an agent of change in the world today.

You will see how compassion has to be personal, something that you actually do for the person who is in front of you and alongside you. Through many personal illustrations and examples and solid scriptural teaching, we show how compassion works best when it is taken from the pew to the street in one-to-one, face-to-face encounters with specific individuals.

Compassion, as you will see, is more than a feeling. Your feelings for others must be backed up by your actions for others. Frederick Buechner said that compassion is the knowledge that there can never really be any peace and joy for me until there is peace and joy finally for you.

Yes, compassion *acts* always bring about positive change in others. We live in a world with many challenges and there is not just one person who can resolve the world's problems. But together we can. As each one of us begins to respond to the compassionate heart of God we can change the world. We will change the world.

We pray these words will challenge you, inspire you, and equip you to go forth in compassion and love.

Heavenly Father, help us to become a compassionate people. Have mercy upon us and change us from glory to glory, that your image might be perfected in us. We want to be like you, Father, and like your only Son, our Lord Jesus Christ. Change our concepts, eradicate our prejudices, demolish our mental strongholds, transform our minds, and give us a strong desire to be merciful and compassionate to all we come in contact with. Let us be agents of change in our world today. In Jesus' name, Amen.

chapter nine

Blessed Are the Poor—Heidi Baker

by
Julia C. Loren

"I'm going to worship and I am going to love."

Heidi Baker,
Voice of the Apostles conference, 2005

"MAMA IDA"

There are those who talk the talk and there are others who walk the walk. Heidi Baker is a modern-day apostle of compassion who is living the call—right now.

Heidi is "mama" to thousands of displaced, abused, and orphaned children who have been raised alongside her own two children, Elisha and Crystalyn. She is truly one who radiates the love, compassion, and joy of the Lord to all she meets. She calls herself a "laid down lover of God"—one whose life is wholly given over to the Lord, one whose life also inspires others to surrender themselves more completely to the love and service of Jesus.

"Fully possessed by the Holy Spirit we become lovers and we do radical things because we know who we are," Heidi said at a Voice of the Apostles conference in 2005.

In a world that glamorizes the achievements of men, Heidi Baker shuns the spotlight. When she speaks at conferences, those attending tend to see and hear more of Jesus and less of her. Her joy is to fade into the background and let Jesus take over. People weep as the Spirit of God tenderizes their hearts with His compassion for the lost, the broken, and the hurting ones all around the world. Fluent in several languages, she is a gifted communicator with advanced educational degrees. She also has seen astounding miracles during her 30 years of ministry, especially in Mozambique, where she and her husband, Rolland, and their Iris Ministries team, have planted more than 7,000 "bush churches," 5 Bible schools, and 4 children's feeding centers since 1990.[1]

Astounding miracles are common to Heidi and Rolland. The blind receive their sight; the deaf hear; and children with AIDS have seroconvert to normalcy. Children traumatized by war, severe neglect and abuse, full of hate, who can barely speak or trust, rapidly responded to their love. Today these same children can be found dancing and ministering with joy. The Baker's have seen God supernaturally multiply food to feed hungry orphans and crowds who gather for meetings. African pastors who have been trained by the Baker's have raised 53 people from the dead in Mozambique—so far.[2]

The Bakers' lives display the full meaning of Jesus' death and resurrection as they embrace the Cross daily—a cross that includes suffering and sacrifice for the sake of releasing healing and reconciling the world to Jesus. It is a cross of compassion and a cross of love.

They spend countless hours soaking in the love of God and interceding for those to whom they minister. Heidi, as a result, has learned that worship is the key to releasing love. And their "intimacy with God provokes confidence that releases faith to stand in God's presence and see Him as big as He is. They live in a place rife with the external evidence of demonic control—war, disease, famine, and corruption. Yet their internal dwelling is "...the place of refuge, a fortress, a secret place of worship and communion. They access a place of blinding, coruscating light. From that place they embark on their mission, to magnify the Lord in the world of men."[3]

HEIDI'S CALLING

Tenacity characterizes this petite, 46-year-old blonde, who is originally from Laguna Beach, California. At age of 16, when most Laguna teens lounged on the beach enjoying the party atmosphere of the era, Heidi was accepted as an American Field Service student. She was sent to a Choctaw Indian reservation in Mississippi, where she was exposed to an environment of poverty that she had never seen before. It was here, that she gave her life to Jesus and, after a 5-day fast, encountered the Lord in a dramatic way.

"On the night of the fifth day, I expectantly went to the Roark's little Pentecostal church in the country and was drawn to the altar. I knelt down and lifted my arms to the Lord. Suddenly, I felt taken to a new heavenly place. Pastor Roark was preaching, but I couldn't hear his loud, powerful voice at all. God's glory came to me again, wrapping me in a pure and brilliant white light. I was overwhelmed by who He is. I had never felt so loved, and I began to weep. This time He spoke to me audibly. 'I am calling you to be a minister and a missionary,' He said. 'You are to go to Africa, Asia, and England.' Again my heart was pounding and racing. I thought I might die.

"Then the Lord Jesus spoke to me and told me I would be married to Him. He kissed my hand, and it felt as if warm oil ran down my arm. I was overcome with love for Him. I knew at that moment that I would go anywhere anytime and say anything for Him. I was ruined for this world by His intense love and mercy in calling me to Himself."[4]

Full of the presence and love of Jesus, Heidi started telling everyone about Him—on the reservation and later, in her high school. She talked the local Episcopal priest into letting her start a Christian coffeehouse in the parish hall and ministered every Friday night for several years—praying for the drug addicts, alcoholics, homeless, and demon-possessed people. In the meanwhile, she attended Southern California College (now Vanguard University).

During her last year in college in 1980, she met her husband, Rolland Baker, grandson of well-known missionaries to China. Missionaries who had gained a place in the Church history books for their vital part in launching a revival among Chinese youth in the pre-Maoist years (see H.A. Baker's *Visions Beyond the Vail*). True to both Rolland's heritage and Heidi's calling, they discerned that they were called together to help bring revival among the poor. Their ministry would be incarnational. They would live like the people, learn the language and the culture from those on the street, suffer with them and earn trust in the process. They married six months later and have since traveled as missionaries to Hong Kong, England, and Mozambique. Their work has extended from Africa into many other countries of the world.

LAUNCHED INTO FIELDS OF POVERTY AND WAR

Their work in Africa began in 1990, when Rolland saw a *Time* magazine article that described the poverty in Mozambique, naming it the poorest country in the world. God knew He needed tenacious and seasoned missionaries and launched them out to start Iris Ministries—working among the Muslims and the poorest of the poor, who were ravished by war, starvation and disease. The following excerpt describes their introduction to the mission field best:[5]

"At the time, the country was involved in a prolonged civil war, and it wasn't until 1995, after a cease-fire was declared between the Renamo (north) and the Frelimo (south), that the Bakers were invited by South African missionaries to go into the war-torn country. They and their friends loaded a few supplies into a red Nissan truck and drove to the border of Mozambique.

"To their dismay, the truck sputtered and lost power until, finally, the engine stopped just in front of the border gate between South Africa and Mozambique.

"Suddenly, helicopters began flying over them, and people started yelling. The truck in front of them was riddled with bullets from bandits. But as soon as the bandits left and the air cleared, the truck the Bakers were in mysteriously started, so they were able to continue their journey to Maputo, the nation's capital.

"The countryside they saw on their way was desolate in the aftermath of the civil war. There were no hospitals or ambulances, but many lay sick or injured as a result of the conflict.

"The Bakers struggled to begin a church and an orphanage in a rundown building. In these grim conditions, the Bakers say God displayed His power over poverty one day by multiplying a small amount of chili and rice—originally intended to feed only four people—to such a degree that it was sufficient for not only the Baker family but also 80 orphaned children."

STOPPING FOR ONE

Stopping for the one child on the street, the one scavenging for food in the dump, the girl languishing under forced prostitution has always been the focus of Heidi's ministry. In the early days after their arrival in Mozambique they took in dozens of children, many of whom were extremely sick, dying, or angry to the point of violence. Some were healed. Others were loved into total emotional, physical, and spiritual health. Others experienced the love of God for a brief time until Heaven called them home.

Currently the Bakers and their team care for thousands of orphans living in several children's centers and in the "foster" homes of pastors and widows. Every Iris Ministries pastor, whether he leads a church in a city or in the bush, is encouraged to adopt at least 10 orphans. Local widows are summoned to feed and care for the overflow of homeless children who flock to the love offered by the Christians. Many of the children have lost their parents to AIDS in a country where more than 180,000 children are AIDS orphans.

An article in *Charisma* magazine describes the differences in the children before and after Heidi's touch:

> Gitou was an AIDS orphan and a tough street kid when Heidi Baker met him. "He said he was 12, but he looked around 8. His heart was hardened, and he continued telling me off whenever I came near," she recalled. "But I just kept loving and loving Gitou until his heart melted. Now he preaches out on the street and leads many to the Lord."

Constancia was a scared little orphan girl of around 5 who was left on the steps of Iris Ministries' orphanage. "She didn't speak and couldn't communicate," Heidi said. "The Lord just told me to chase her...with His love. I'd chase her and hold her until she fell asleep in my arms."

"The same day Constancia was baptized; she began to speak and even asked to lead the choir. She told us then that she'd been mute since seeing her parents brutally murdered right in front of her."[6]

Ever praying about what to do with the overwhelming needs of so many thousands of children and the growing ministry, Heidi received an amazing strategy from the Lord.

"The Lord had showed me thousands and thousands of children, and I believe we are called to care for millions of children. At first I was absolutely overwhelmed with that vision, and I thought, "God how could that ever happen? How could we ever do that, just stopping for the one? I don't know how we could ever, ever do that." I was praying, crying, fasting and asking God, and He said that He would bring a great revival, and in this revival He would touch the hearts of pastors, and they would become fathers of the fatherless. He said that was His answer for these children. They would be literally cared for by these Mozambican pastors. And then He told me that the widows would cook for them and feed them, that the widows would help farm and that we were to build indigenous buildings made of mud and straw, buildings that fit in with every church. We would see these children cared for in families."[7]

FROM STRUGGLING MISSIONARY TO APOSTOLIC ANOINTING

Heidi and Rolland labored for years in Africa; this lifestyle eventually took a toll on Heidi's spirit. Her ever-expanding heart of love ached to do more.

"Now in Africa we were seeing the sequel to the revival Rolland's grandfather saw among his orphans in China. That was not an isolated outpouring without further fruit. In it Rolland and I saw the heart of

God. We saw how He feels about the lost and forgotten. We saw how He delights to use the helpless and hopeless to accomplish His best work. We saw His pleasure in revealing Himself to those humble and poor in spirit enough to appreciate Him. We saw His ability to use simple children to ignite revival. Now we are seeing Him do the same thing in Mozambique. And what He was doing in our children's center fired our appetites all the more for revival.

"We were simply desperate for more of God.

"In January of 1998, Randy Clark was [in Toronto] preaching about the apostolic anointing, laying down our lives and the holy fire of God. He pointed to me and said, 'God is asking, Do you want Mozambique?' I experienced the heavenly fire of God falling on me. I was so hot I literally thought I was going to burn up and die. I remember crying out, 'Lord, I'm dying!' I heard the Lord clearly speak to my heart, 'Good, I want you to be dead!' He wanted me to be completely emptied of self so He could pour even more of His Spirit into my life.

"For seven days I was unable to move. Rolland had to pick me up and carry me. I had to be carried to the washroom, to the hotel and back to the meeting. The weight of His glory was upon me. I felt so heavy that I could not lift my head."[8]

Unable to speak or move for seven days, the presence of God changed Heidi's life. She had never felt so humbled, poor, and vulnerable. Engulfed in the presence of the Lord, she listened as God spoke to her about relinquishing control of her life and the ministry to Him. He spoke of planting hundreds of churches in Mozambique. Where Heidi and Rolland labored for several years with seemingly little fruit, God would explode His power and unleash His presence over the region.

"It had taken us seventeen years to plant four churches, and two of them were pretty weak. As I lay there, engulfed in His presence, He spoke to me about hundreds of churches being planted in Mozambique. I remember laughing hysterically, thinking I would have to be two hundred years old before that promise was fulfilled!

"God showed me that I needed to learn to work with the rest of His Body....

"I thought I had been depending on Him to plant churches, when in reality I depended a lot on my own abilities. Naturally, things moved pitifully slowly. It's comical to think we can do God's work for Him. It's all grace. He allows us to participate with Him, and so there is always enough. He showed me how much I needed Him and the Body of Christ. He is calling us to complete humility and gentleness. It is never about us; it is always about Him."[9]

After that transforming encounter everything in Heidi's ministry changed. She returned to Mozambique and began releasing people into ministry, recognizing potential ministers even in young children. She relinquished control and started delegating responsibilities. In return came the apostolic anointing to heal the sick, cast out demons, raise the dead, see blind eyes open and deaf ears hear, to train and launch hundreds of pastors into the largely Muslim fields of Mozambique, where they had labored for years to plant a handful of churches they were shocked to discover the Lord empowering them to plant thousands more in record time.

KEYS TO FRUITFULNESS

The Bakers say that one of the keys to becoming a successful ministry lies in relinquishing complete control to God, a concept the Western church needs to learn in order to sow effective ministry throughout the earth.

Another key to fruitfulness, the couple says, is intimacy with God. "Revival breaks out when people are desperate for God. When they become intimate with Him and lose sight of themselves, then anything can happen," says Rolland Baker.

One of the most important keys to sustaining successful ministry, however, is tenacious faith to persevere through opposition

Heidi and Rolland Baker articulate the price they pay as they come against the demonic strongholds—a price that includes theft of ministry resources, sickness, malicious lies, and political backlash. They have faced guns and violence. Not one New Creation Power Broker on the mission field today leads an easy life coasting along in a bullet-proof bubble of the Holy Spirit, untouched by human suffering and demonic attack. They need the miraculous power of God to touch every life.

A CHALLENGING PERSPECTIVE

The Bakers' mission field perspective: "Some who hear us in conferences may come away with the impression that we lead a charmed, tribulation-free life of endless miracles! We do prefer to give Jesus and His glorious power most of the attention in our ministry, but it may encourage you to know that, like Paul, we are jars of clay who glory also in our weakness. When we are weak, then we are strong (2 Cor. 12:10). We do encounter fierce, demonic opposition, and its intensity is almost incomprehensible. This Mozambican province where we live has been a pagan, occultic stronghold for centuries, and the evil we encounter shocks us over and over. Our time, energy, funds, and resources are viciously attacked and drained as the devil aims to turn our hearts away from this great revival in which God has graciously placed us.

"Together with Paul, we understand that these things happen that we might not rely on ourselves but on God, who raises the dead (2 Cor. 1:9). We resist the devil by overcoming evil with good, and by resting in Him with all the more faith and childlike joy. We cannot lose while secure in His heart. We have no need to shield ourselves, but we entrust our souls to a faithful Creator in doing what is right (1 Peter 4:19). The God who has raised at least 53 people from the dead among our churches in Africa will also renew and refresh us with His incomparable power. He will not fail us; we are His workmanship!"[10]

It is their tenacious faith that enabled them to remain in Mozambique long enough to see a breakthrough, not only in church plants, but in increasing miracles as this report in *Charisma* magazine (2006) reveals:

> The miracles are a big part of the Bakers' method for winning Muslims to Jesus. Heidi says they do it "by signs, wonders, and caring for the orphan and the widow. It's love and stopping for the one."

> According to her report, however, their target audience is not immediately receptive. "At first the Muslims throw rocks," she says, "but once they see signs and wonders and practical love they can't resist. My ministry team are 8-, 10- and 12-year-olds. Barefoot children in raggedy shirts lay hands on the crippled and they walk."

Recently, Heidi took some of these children with her to minister to synchronistic Muslims. "They're not a happy bunch," she says. "My kids were ducking rocks, and one hit me low in the back. I jumped up and said: 'Bring me the deaf! Bring me the blind!'"

The team was led through the darkness to an old man who was both lame and blind. He got saved and then said, "I have a headache."

The Bakers' children prayed over him. He was still blind and crippled. Heidi told him, "When you are healed tomorrow, send me a runner."

Heidi returned to their meeting place and again asked, "Anybody else blind?" A blind man was brought to her and she said, "I bless him in the name of Jesus." Heidi says when the blind man screamed, "Ahhhhh! I can see!" the villagers finally stopped throwing rocks.

The next day, Heidi says, a runner came up to the car she was sitting in with the Muslim man who owns Pemba and reported: "The blind man can see! He's at his farm working."

The owner of Pemba grabbed Heidi's hand and stuck it on his head, tears running down his face. "Pray for me!" he said.

The explosive growth of their ministry is due to the miraculous power that God has released through them in the past decade. The Gospel is advancing whole villages at a time as the Holy Spirit's power is poured out—resulting in healing released through compassion and love.

FAITH FOR HEALING

Heidi's faith for healing and refreshing has been tested over and over again and she has persevered to help bring healing to others. She has even struggled to receive God's healing for a recurrent staph infection.

In 2006, Heidi lay dying from a methicillin-resistant staph infection in a hospital in Johannesburg, South Africa. It was her seventh hospitalization for the infection doctors attributed to her work among the street children. Her two children, away in the U.S. attending a ministry school, stood vigil in prayer. Rolland cancelled his commitments to remain by her side and sent out urgent requests for corporate prayer. But Heidi had already decided that, like the apostle Paul, although she would love to be with the Lord, it would be better for her to remain in the flesh and continue the work of the ministry. And, characteristically of her tenacious faith, she cried out, "I'm not going out like this!"

This report from *Charisma* magazine (2006) summarizes her miraculous recovery from that last, life-threatening bout with the infection:

> Heidi checked herself out of the hospital two times. The first time she flew to Pemba, Africa, where hundreds of Mozambicans came to the airport to greet her and sing and dance for her healing. Although she was experiencing incredible pain, she preached to a tent full of people from the Makua and Makonde tribes.

> That evening, 55 Makua ran forward to give their lives to Jesus. The Bakers were thrilled with the souls saved, but Heidi's body remained wracked with pain, and following the meeting she flew back to Johannesburg for further treatment.

> After returning to the hospital and taking antibiotics for another month, Heidi still had not recovered. The doctors told Heidi there were more advanced drugs in California—her only hope for healing.

> Heidi packed her bags and told the medical staff, "I'm going to see a Specialist in Toronto."

> She checked herself out of the hospital for the second time and flew to Toronto, to the Toronto Airport Christian Fellowship, home of what is now known as the Toronto Blessing. Heidi lay on the floor with a pillow, soaking in the presence of God, too sick to get up and participate in worship.

> When it was time for her to preach, she felt she had to stand. Weakened and suffering with intense pain, she began her message from Zechariah.

"The fire of God pulsated through my body," Heidi says. "I was literally healed as I preached. There was no pain by the end of the service—it disappeared."

At the end of the meeting, Heidi danced across the platform in thanksgiving to God. Rolland claims tenacity is part of the DNA of a good missionary. "If faith is not exciting to you, don't sign up," he says.

Heidi agrees. "Tenacity is part of the kingdom. King Jesus will win, and we stand on His side."

THE FUTURE IS JESUS

Rather than burning out (physically and spiritually) on the mission field and giving up, or being consumed with worry over funds and food shortages, rather than flickering out in middle age after decades of ministry, Heidi and Rolland are burning ever stronger, completely dependant on God. Heidi has come to know of the love of God more keenly through the suffering orphans they minister to daily, orphans who reflect the face and heart of God.

"It is a privilege beyond price to see the joy and affection of the Holy Spirit poured out like a waterfall on people who have known so much severe hardship, disappointment and bitter loneliness in their lives," Baker wrote recently in her online ministry report.

"From the freezing cold gypsy huts of eastern Bulgaria to the 115 degree heat of Sudanese refugee camps, from the isolated native Inuits of arctic Canada to the dirt-poor subsistence farmers along the Zambezi River, we see ravenous desire for God among the poor and lowly. Jesus knows their suffering, and He will make it up to them. He will be their God, and they will be His people. He will use them to shame the wise and make the world jealous of their wealth toward Him."

As for how the Lord is using Heidi, she, too is shaming the wise and making the world recognize that compassion releases the anointing of Jesus. As a laid down lover of God, anything is possible.

"I'm so desperate to stay in this place of abandonment. From this place, nothing is impossible. I have only one message—passion and compassion. We're passionate lovers of God, so that we become absolutely nothing. His love fills us. When it's time to stand up, God stands up with us. We focus on His face, never on our ministry, anointing, or numbers.

"All I want to do is love God and care for His people. I find them in the garbage, under trees dying of AIDS. I'm just really simple. Jesus said, 'Look into my eyes,' and everything completely changed. His eyes are filled with love and passion and compassion. Jesus always stops for the dying man, the dying woman and the dying child. That's all I know, passion and compassion. He calls me to love every single person I see every single day.

"Just focus on His face. You will only make it to the end if you can focus on His face. Focus on His beautiful face. You can't feed the poor, you can't go to the street, you can't see anything happen unless you see His face. One glance of His eyes, and we have all it takes to lie down. We're not afraid to die."[11]

LAID DOWN LOVERS

Having led intercessory and equipping teams on site in Mozambique to co-labor with Iris Ministries, I can give you a firsthand report. I agree with John Crowder's statement in his marvelous book, *Miracle Workers, Reformers, and The New Mystics*, "Heidi has no formula for raising the dead except that she literally loves people back to life. She has held the dead bodies of babies and others, weeping over them for hours, until warmth came back into them and they were supernaturally revived."[12] This indeed is compassion in action.

As she globe trots the nations spreading the fire of the Father's great love, often you can hear Heidi devotionally singing a song that pierces your heart. *"I want to be a laid down lover!"* Want to join the song?

> *Dear Lord God Almighty, Thank you for the strength and courage you have given those who are laid down lovers of you. Thank you for those who reach out to the poor—one child, one person at a time. Help us to become like those who seek to help and comfort. We need your face before us to focus on and to draw power from—we need you to show us the way. In the precious name of Jesus, Amen.*

ENDNOTES

1. Lee Grady, "Heidi Baker's Uncomfortable Message to America," *Charisma* magazine, August 2006.

2. Ibid.

3. Julia Loren, *Shifting Shadows of Supernatural Power* (Shippensburg, PA: Destiny Image Publishers, 2006), 91.

4. Baker and Baker, *There is Always Enough* (Grand Rapids, MI: Chosen Books, 2002), 26.

5. C. Hope Flinchbaugh, "Brave Hearts in a Desperate Land," *Charisma* magazine, March 2006.

6. Josie Newman, "Miracles and Church Growth Mark Mozambique Ministry," *Charisma* magazine, March 2004.

7. Baker and Baker, *There is Always Enough*, 160.

8. Ibid., 67-68.

9. Ibid., 68-69.

10. Julia Loren, *Shifting Shadows*, 108.

11. Baker and Baker, *There is Always Enough*, 176-177.

12. John Crowder, *Miracle Workers, Reformers, and The New Mystics,* (Shippensburg, PA: Destiny Image Publishers, 2006), 147.

chapter ten

It's Got To Be Personal

by

James W. Goll

But you, beloved, building yourselves up on your most holy faith, praying in the Holy Spirit, keep yourselves in the love of God, looking for the mercy of our Lord Jesus Christ unto eternal life. And on some have compassion, making a distinction (Jude 20-22 NKJV).

I grew up in a rural area of Missouri, and now I reside in a beautiful country setting in Tennessee with my family. Because of my background of living in rural, agricultural areas, I know something about seed time and harvest. From that vantage point, I realize that there is great power in the hidden seeds that are planted in God's good earth.

Under the direction of my parents, along with my sisters, I helped plant many gardens during the spring of each year. Later, in July and August, I weeded many rows of corn, potatoes, green beans, tomatoes, and many other colorful and leafy vegetables.

I often wondered why I had to work so hard in the hot and humid weather, but when fall and winter arrived, I understood and appreciated why I did so. My mom made some of the best vegetable soup, which I and many others, greatly enjoyed. To this day, I can still taste the luscious flavor of her homemade soup, and I can still smell its enticing aroma which filled the entire house.

I learned a great deal from the principle of seedtime and harvest from those garden experiences, and later in life found it to be one of the major guiding biblical principles, as well.

Michal Ann also enjoyed the bounty of large gardens when she was growing up. In addition to this, her dad loved using his old cider press to make apple and pear cider. In order to make those delicious, natural beverages, however, one first needs fruit. So Michal Ann and the rest of her family would go into the orchards of the Midwest and pick the fruits her father needed to make his favorite recipe. In fact, the Willard family song that is still sung at family gatherings is the "Johnny Appleseed Song." In harmonious unity they sing with all their hearts, giving glory and thanks to God for the harvest He has provided.

SEEDS OF COMPASSION

Our job, as believers, is to plant seeds of compassion in a personal way wherever we go in much the same way that John Chapman ("Johnny Appleseed") planted seeds from apples throughout the United States during the late 18th century. Every fall we now enjoy the fruits of his labor and commitment in the form of apple pies, apple sauce, apple butter, apple cider, and apple cobbler. Wouldn't a nice slice of apple pie a la mode taste good right now?

Before I make you too hungry, though, let's go on to look at some spiritual principles associated with springtime and harvest, planting, and sowing. We plant the seeds, and God gives the harvest. This is just as true in the spiritual realm as it is in the natural. As we sow seeds of compassion into the lives of others, we look to God to water, cultivate, groom, and prune the emerging seedlings so they will bring forth fruitfulness in due season in the lives of those to whom we minister. There is phenomenal power in the hidden seed.

Sharon Salzberg writes, "Any ordinary favor we do for someone or any compassionate reaching out may seem to be going nowhere at first, but may be planting a seed we can't see right now. Sometimes we need to just do the best we can and then trust in an unfolding we can't design or ordain."[1]

In one of my favorite verses Paul points out that God will supply the seed for you: *"And [God] Who provides seed for the sower and bread for eating will also provide and multiply your [resources for] sowing and increase the fruits of your righteousness [which manifest itself in active goodness, kindness, and charity]" (2 Cor. 9:10). The psalmist David adds for us, "He has scattered abroad his gifts to the poor, his righteousness endures forever; his horn will be lifted high in honor"* (Ps. 112:9 NIV).

If your intention is to know God and serve Him by ministering to others, He will supply your seed to sow. He will make His all-sufficient grace abound toward you, and He will multiply your resources. From His seed fruit will grow—the fruit that is called "the fruit of the Spirit." (See Galatians 5:22-23.) And there will be a harvest. You can count on that. But, remember, the seedlings of love are what will bring a great reward.

CHAMPIONS OF FAITH, HOPE, AND LOVE

The Holy Spirit is looking for champions in our day. Michal Ann and I have written about several of these valiant heroes in the *Women on the Front Lines* series in which the book you are now reading is the third volume.

There are many champions—both great and small—who have made it into "God's Hall of Heroes." Some of these good people we may never meet nor know until we see them in Heaven, but others, such as Rolland and Heidi Baker of Iris Ministries are modern-day trailblazers and pacesetters from whom each of us can learn a great deal.

All too often we focus on the gigantic exploits that are done by great people of faith, but we must never forget that little acts of love and kindness often precede public displays of power. Each of us must go through a hidden preparation period in which we learn how to walk in compassion and, as in any process we have to take "baby steps" at first. This is the seed-planting stage.

Michal Ann and I have had the pleasure of knowing Mahesh and Bonnie Chavda for many years. As many already know, it was the healing prayers of Mahesh Chavda, which paved the way for the Lord to bless us with our four beautiful children. I have often said, "Mahesh is not a show horse; he is a work horse!"

In the earlier days of my ministry I had the privilege of doing some behind-the-scenes work for Mahesh's meetings as he traveled around the United States and internationally. I remember getting drinks for him, serving as a "catcher," fetching his tennis shoes so his tired feet could be more comfortable after praying with people until 2 A.M., and enjoying the fun of non-religious fellowship with him.

What always impressed me the most, as I observed and learned from Mahesh, was how he always took time for each individual. He never seemed to be in a rush; he ministered to each person as though every single individual was the most important person in the meetings. The Baker's and the Chavda's are both great, modern day examples of the power of taking time for the one—always making it personal. The following is a story that was taken from Mahesh's first book, *Only Love Can Make a Miracle*. It shows how his heart of compassion and his ministry began to bloom.

ONLY LOVE CAN MAKE A MIRACLE

"The Lord gave me an overwhelming love for children. It was hard to explain. It was as though the Lord broke off a little piece of His heart and placed it inside me. I loved those children as though they were my own.

"I used to work a nine-hour shift in Lily, usually with the ambulatory children, those who were able to get around on their own. When I was off duty, I would go to the non-ambulatory wards just to be with the children there. I had such a love for them. The thought of them having to spend the rest of their lives in those cribs almost broke my heart.

"I knew that God loved them, too, and that he wanted to channel that love through me. I didn't really know what to do with them or even how to pray for them. I used to just hold them and pray quietly in the Spirit. Often I would sit in a rocking chair with one of them for hours, just praying and singing in tongues.

"One little girl especially touched my heart. Her name was Laura. Laura's mother had been using hard drugs during pregnancy, and she had been born blind and severely retarded. I used to rotate through the different non-ambulatory wards on my after-hours visits, but in time I began to gravitate more and more to little Laura. She was so precious to me.

"One day I had occasion to go into Laura's ward during the day. It had been several weeks since I had started holding her and praying with her. As I approached her crib, she turned toward me and stretched out her hands to welcome me! There were a number of staff members nearby. They were amazed. They kept saying to each other, 'Did you see that?' Laura had never shown any outward response to anyone before, not even to being touched. Now she was responding to me from across the room. Could it be that she was gaining her sight? Could it be that the Lord was healing her through my prayers?

"Not long after this, I had a similar experience with a little boy who had been born with a terrible birth defect. His spine was deformed so that he was unable to sit up. Again, after I had been praying with him over a period of several weeks, he suddenly became able to sit up. His back was healed!

"As far as I can recall, I never once specifically prayed that these children be healed. I had prayed that way for my mother because I felt the Lord had told me to. Other than that, prayer for healing was not something I was accustomed to doing.

"When I was with the children, I would simply hold them and pray that the Lord would somehow enable them to experience His love through me. I was as surprised as anyone when they started getting better.

"I was learning many lessons in my school of the Spirit. Now I was learning that the power of God was to be found in the love of God. When the Lord sent me to the State School, he did not say, 'I am sending you as my ambassador of power or of miracles.' He said, 'I am sending you as my ambassador of love.' That was the way I saw myself and that was the way I prayed for the children: that the Lord would make His love real to them. The healings came almost as a by-product. I learned that only love can make a miracle."[2]

Will you be an ambassador of love for the Father? His love is powerful; it truly is the stuff of which miracles are made.

REVIVAL OF KINDNESS

The world needs a revival of kindness today. Imagine what would happen if God's people began to use their innate creativity to develop ways to show kindness to others. Simple acts of kindness, stemming from the love of God, would effect major changes in people's lives.

Early one morning I was awakened by the voice of the Holy Spirit speaking to me. The dove of God opened my left ear and was gently whispering secrets to me. I remember so well, hearing of coming moves of His manifested presence with signs and wonders and displays of great power. But what stuck with me the most that morning was one simple phrase, "I will have a revival of kindness."

After the experience was over, I wrote the content down in a journal that laid by my bedside. Later I shared this precious encounter with my wife, Michal Ann. She mused and pondered on the thought. It went deep within her very being—"I will have a revival of kindness." Perhaps this experience was one of those seeds that put language to what was already growing in Michal Ann's heart. Today, she along with a company of other desperate lovers, have launched a new ministry aptly entitled Compassion Acts.

I wonder what our culture and society would really look like if instead of the hurried dog eat dog frantic pace of getting and staying ahead, we actually took time to pause, breathe, and act a little more like Jesus? Recently, I had one of those piercing, instructional dreams when the voice of the Lord came to me. I heard, "You're never too old for the sermon on the Mount." Take some pauses along the way—take time for the one and demonstrate compassion. Be the Sermon on the Mount to another.

RANDOM ACTS OF KINDNESS

I wonder what a revival of kindness looks like? We know of some of the characteristics of power evangelism and crusade evangelism by reading and observing the great revivals of the past. But it seems to Michal Ann and me, that for a genuine revival of kindness to come to pass—it has to be personal!

In fact, I believe the Holy Spirit wants us to have some fun in the process. Why not try some "random acts of kindness" as seeds to sow. Here are some random acts of kindness that you might want to consider as you go about your daily routine.

- While going through a toll booth, pay the toll for the driver in the car behind you.

- Give someone a word of encouragement.

- While in the drive-through line of a fast-food restaurant, pay for the meals that were ordered by the people behind you.

- Take time to be a good listener to someone who needs to share his or her circumstances with you.

- Get trained and participate in the Healing Rooms in your area.

- Distribute Bibles and Christian books to people you encounter in your day-to-day activities.

- Randomly give out worship CDs to young people in a mall.

- Surrender your place in line to someone who seems to be in a hurry, whether in a supermarket, a bank, or elsewhere.

- Participate in an outreach with Dream Teams at public venues.

- Ask others if you could pray for them and invite the Holy Spirit's presence to come so that God's glory will be revealed!

- Give an unusually good tip to a server in a restaurant and leave them a note telling them that God cares.

- Take bags of groceries to a poor family and leave a note that says, "From the Man Upstairs who sees and cares."

- Invite international college students to your home over the holidays.

- Send cards of encouragement and comfort to those alone.

- Invite people to attend church or a time of fellowship with you.

- Tell people in practical ways about the love of Jesus.

All of these "random acts" of kindness are seeds of compassion that will truly make a difference in the lives of others. Take a moment now and see if you can come up with other ways to express God's love in personal, practical, and tangible ways. Hey, I've got another idea—don't just make a list—add works to your faith and do something. Yes, let's do something for Jesus sake!

TRUE COMPASSION IS ALWAYS PERSONAL

Compassion is always personal. It costs you something and it releases something. In *Webster's New Collegiate Dictionary* we learn that compassion is "a sympathetic consciousness of others' distress together with a desire to alleviate it." It is more than just a feeling; it is also an action. Compassion gives you an insight into another's need and it enables you to understand their hurts, pain, and heartache.

God will reveal to you what needs to be done to help alleviate another's situation.

Vine's Expository Dictionary of New Testament Words provides us with many additional insights related to compassion by showing us the Greek verbs that are associated with it:

Oikteiro—to have pity, a feeling of distress through the ills of others. This verb is used to describe the compassion of God, which is one of His central attributes. As you can see, God's compassion is always personal and it is directed to individuals in need.

Splanchnizomai—to be moved as within one's inwards; to be moved with compassion, and to yearn with compassion. This is the verb that is frequently used to describe the way Jesus was moved with compassion toward the multitudes and toward individuals.

Do you remember the story of the widow of Nain? Her only son had died. When

Jesus saw her, "*...He had compassion on her and said to her, 'Do not weep.'*" (Luke 7:13).

The Lord saw the funeral procession for the young man, and He was moved with compassion for the widow who was experiencing a painful sense of loss.

Notice the progression here: first, He *saw*; then He was *moved* with compassion. But it didn't stop there. It went beyond the feeling level and became an act.

Jesus' primary concern in this example did not appear to be the eternal state of the young man; rather, He was concerned about the mother and what she was going through. He felt compassion for her.

Not only did He tell her, *"Don't weep,"* but He also took positive steps to rectify the situation. The Bible says, *"He went forward and touched the funeral bier,...And He said, 'Young man, I say to you, arise [from death]!'"* (Luke 7:14).

Jesus saw. Jesus felt compassion. Jesus spoke words of comfort. Then Jesus moved forward with a touch and a command. The result was: *"And the man [who was] dead sat up and began to speak. And [Jesus] gave him [back] to his mother"* (Luke 7:15).

First, we have to perceive (see) the need. Then we speak words of encouragement and comfort, which may often lead us to communicate love and warmth through a touch or an embrace. Next, we take action by doing what we can to provide practical help and assistance to the person in need. One thing we can always do is to pray for him or her, and, as Tennyson said, "More things are wrought by prayer than this world dreams of."

AN ERUPTION OF MERCY

Deep within His spirit, Jesus is always in tune with the Father. His intimacy with His Father propelled Him to go out among the people and to be sensitive to their needs. In other words, He looked outside Himself and He saw what others needed. We can do the same, but, first, we must spend time alone with God in the secret place of the Most High. That is time well-spent, for it empowers us to go forth in love and compassion.

A deep yearning arises as we spend time with the Father, and this yearning is focused on helping others.

In his book, *Authority to Heal*, Ken Blue tells us that Jesus' compassion for people was not merely an expression of His will, but rather an eruption from deep within His being.[3] This volcanic image shows us how compassion should work in each of our lives, as an eruption of sympathy, empathy, and mercy flowing out to others like lava from a crater. God's mercies are everlasting and they are constantly flowing from His throne—a throne that is established on the foundation of righteousness and mercy.

Have you ever noticed that when you get emotional about something, you do something in response to your emotions? When your emotions are stirred up, you take action. You may weep, jump up and down, write a letter, or head in a certain direction with a specific goal in mind. It is the same with God. He gets emotional over us, and it stirs Him to take action on our behalf.

Some things stick with you. I remember so very well many of the journeys I have taken as an intercessory missionary praying on site with insight. Walking in the city of Solei in impoverished Haiti...how can I forget? The sights, the sounds and yes, the smells...

As I walked through the areas where little boys wore no clothes, where there were no flushing toilets or anything close to it for that matter, my heart broke. I walked in areas that were not safe to be according to the World Health Organization standards. But God propelled my feet to walk among the poor, praying, caring...and sowing seeds of kindness. I wept as I walked among these precious people. I flat out had a compassion eruption that motivated me to go back and forth numerous times from the United States to Haiti, the Pearl of the Antilles, hoping, praying and longing to somehow make a difference.

Do you want to walk where Jesus did? Then watch out—that desire echoed before God, might just take you into some really strange and wonderful places! Could it be that the farther we go on our journey with God, the more He wants us to be like Him? Do you want to be like Him? Do you want to follow in the footsteps of the Lord? Do you want His image to be formed in you?

If your answer to these questions is yes, then you must let the necessary ingredient of compassion fill your heart and motivate you to get on the frontlines of service for your Lord. God is full of compassion and His eruptions of love and mercy are yearning to be activated in our lives.

SWEETER THAN HONEY

Many people do not understand the nature of God—that He is full of mercy and compassion. If we truly understood this, wouldn't it change everything about us? Wouldn't it impel us to get compassionately involved with meeting others' needs, as Jesus was? Jesus certainly understood what is in the Father's heart, and because He does, He was willing and able to go to the Cross for us.

Such is the task for God's Generals. As forerunning pioneers they die to self and live unto God. Often they open up spiritual truths for us so that those who follow can enter into the fullness of their revelation in teaching and application. John Wimber was a forerunner who was given a simple yet profound revelation from the Father concerning His heart of mercy. Earlier we glanced at a vision that he received, but now I want to develop it in full.

Once while driving his car in southern California, John was given a spiritual vision:

"It really works, I thought as I wended my way towards home, and God used me as a vehicle of his healing mercy. Then I was jolted out of my jubilant mood by an incredible vision. Suddenly in my mind's eye there appeared to be a cloud bank superimposed across the sky, but I had never seen a cloud bank like this one, so I pulled my car over to the side of the road to take a closer look. Then I realized it was not a cloud bank, it was a honeycomb with honey dripping out onto people below. The people were in a variety of postures. Some were reverent; they were weeping and holding their hands out to catch the honey and taste it, even inviting others to take some of their honey. Others acted irritated, wiping the honey off, and complaining about the mess. I was awestruck. Not knowing what to think, I prayed, 'Lord, what is it?'

"He said, 'It's My mercy, John. For some people it's a blessing, but to others it's a hindrance. There is plenty for everyone. Don't ever beg me for healing again. The problem isn't on my end, John. It's down there.'

"That was a moving and profound experience; certainly it revolutionized my life more than any other experience I had since becoming a Christian. I have never looked at healing the same way since that day.

"What made this experience so powerful was that it confirmed my newfound conviction, rooted in Scripture, that God's abundant grace included divine healing, if only we would believe him for it. I learned this lesson from the story in Mark 9:14-32 of Christ healing a man's son who was possessed by a spirit and as a consequence was mute. After the disciples had failed to heal the boy, the father approached Jesus asking if he could help. Jesus wasted no time in identifying the reason for the disciples' failure: unbelief.

"After explaining to Jesus that his son had been possessed by a spirit since childhood, the man asked, '...*But if you can do anything, take pity on us and help us'* (v. 22). Jesus said, *'If you can? Everything is possible for him who believes'* (v. 23). The key to experiencing God's healing mercy was belief, belief in the God who heals. *'I do believe, the father said. Help me overcome my unbelief!'* (v. 24). With this confession, what Jesus called faith as small as a mustard seed in Matthew 17:20, he cast a deaf and mute spirit out of the boy, and the boy was instantly healed.

"What God showed me through Scriptures like Mark 9, my first healing, and the honeycomb vision was that he is much greater than I ever imagined him to be, and with only the smallest act of faith I could experience his compassion and mercy.

"I also realized that God's mercy is constantly falling on us, because everything that He does is related to what He is: the Father of compassion (mercies, *oiktirmos*) and the God of all comfort, who comforts us in all our troubles. (2 Cor. 1:3; Exod. 34:6; Neh. 9:17).

"Psalm 145:9 says, *'The Lord is good to all; he has compassion on all he has made.'* Titus 3:5 says, *'The Lord saves us because of his mercy.'*

"But too often I did not see God in the fullness of his mercy and grace. I trusted him to lead me, but I did not trust him to provide for me; I had faith to receive forgiveness of sins and salvation, but I had no faith for divine healing. I never realized God's mercy was as readily and abundantly available to me as the honey was available to all under the honeycomb.

"Through the honeycomb vision I also understood that my first healing was only the beginning of my experiencing God's mercy if I would only choose to believe and to receive it. In the vision, some people rejoiced, freely received, and freely gave away. The more they gave away, the more they received. 'There is plenty for everyone,' the Lord said. 'Don't ever beg me for healing again.'

"But others, full of unbelief and skepticism, could not receive the grace, blessings, and gifts of God. They could not see that God's mercy and healing are greater than their understanding of how he works. 'The problem isn't on my end,' the Lord said. 'It's down there.' It is we, not God, who place limitations and unbelief on God's compassion and mercy. We are invited to cooperate with his Spirit by entering into a divine partnership, a partnership in which he brings direction and provides for healing."[4]

Faith is integral to our moving out in compassion to the needy people who are all around us. God wants us to minister to people who have unmet needs, unhealed hurts, and unresolved issues in their lives, and He supplies us with the love and power to do so in ways that will actually bring about change.

WANT TO MAKE A DIFFERENCE?

Do you want to make a difference in the world? Then be different from others by walking in compassion wherever you are. Plant seeds of mercy in soil of desperate people's lives. People will see the difference, and they will want to have what you have. Not only that, but they will receive what they need through the grace on your life.

But compassion always has to be personal. It needs to flow from your heart to the person in front of you. As the writer of one the shortest books in the Bible states, *"And on some have compassion, making a distinction"* (Jude 22 NKJV).

We need a revelation of what compassion really is and what it entails. The God of all compassion and comfort wants us to be compassionate in and through you. He lives within you, so let Him and His miracle-working love and compassion flow forth from you. In fact, let compassion have its eruption in your life and propel you, along with a throng of others, into action!

Jesus, be big in me! Let your emotions within me be stirred up. By Your grace, I choose to sow seeds of Your radical transforming love and mercy into the lives of others. I volunteer freely to be a part of Your compassionate army walking throughout the nations to bring a revival of kindness. I want to make a difference! Here I am—use me! Amen and Amen!

ENDNOTES

1. Sharon Salzberg, "The Power of Intention," *O Magazine,* January 2004.

2. Mahesh Chavda, *Only Love Can make a Miracle* (Ann Arbor, MI: Vine Books, Servant Publications), 72-73.

3. Ken Blue, *The Authority to Heal* (Downers Grove, IL: Inter Varsity Press, 1987).

4. John Wimber and Kevin Springer, *Power Healing* (San Francisco, CA: Harper, 1987), 47-48.

chapter eleven

Compassion Acts

by
Michal Ann Goll

Thus has the Lord of hosts spoken: Execute true judgement and show mercy and kindness and tender compassion, every man to his brother. And oppress not the widow or the fatherless, the temporary resident or the poor, and let none of you devise or imagine, or think evil against his brother in your heart (Zechariah 7:9-10).

FACE-TO-FACE AND HEART-TO-HEART

OK—time to breathe! We have journeyed through the Scripture, studying God's heart for justice, righteousness, and mercy. We have looked—up close and personal—at the lives of some amazing women and their impact on the world. Now, it's time to really get personal. Before we go any further though, we are going to rest. Rest is a very important key, especially in regard to this call to compassion. As we open our hearts to feel God's heart, we may feel pressure to "do" something. Where is this pressure coming from? Is it direction from God, or are we beginning to see legitimate needs, but moving out of our mental, or soulish strength rather than out of our spirit? Ah, this is very important!

Take time right now, to stop and rest. Let your mind and heart center on His presence and worship Him for just a few minutes.

Compassion ministry, or whatever you want to call it, can be very draining, and exhausting. But it doesn't have to be. It depends on your motivation and your approach. It should not drive you, but rather, God's heart should lead you. Do you see the difference?

MARY AND MARTHA

Do you remember the story about Mary and Martha? In the past, I heard that "Mary chose the better part," and that Martha was reprimanded.

We need to look at the Scripture again. Part of the story takes place in John 11, and it revolves around Lazarus, who was Mary and Martha's brother. Mary was the one who had anointed Jesus' feet with perfume and wiped His feet with her hair. She was also the one who just wanted to sit at His feet and listen to Him speak, while Martha was in the kitchen, preparing food (see Luke 10:38-39). There has been a lot of emphasis on Mary in recent years, and the place in God she typifies. We all need to have the heart Mary, loving to sit at His feet, period.

Martha, dear Martha! She was the one who received Jesus and welcomed Him into her house. Now, she did become distracted with much serving, and that was the point that Jesus spoke tenderly to her, redirecting her heart to "the better part," to worship Him. (See Luke 10:40.) But I believe He was wooing her, drawing her to Himself, not correcting or belittling her. She had messed up, had an attitude problem, and had compared her serving and cooking to Mary's "sitting." What a common error that is—a lesson we are still trying to learn.

When Lazarus was sick (see John 11), the sisters sent word to Jesus. Jesus loved Lazarus, but He did not come right away, but rather waited until Lazarus died. By the time He came, Lazarus had been in the tomb for four days. Look at John 11:20-22, *"When Martha heard that Jesus was coming, she went to meet Him, while Mary remained sitting in the house. Martha then said to Jesus; Master; if You had been here, my brother would not have died. And even now I know that whatever You ask from God, He will grant it to You."*

Do you see a pattern here? Not only was it Martha who welcomed Jesus into her house, and in that, to her city, but when her brother died, she was the one who met Him, and asked for her brother's life to be restored. We need Martha! It doesn't have to be, "Are you a Mary or a Martha?" The point is, God wants us to be both. There is no place for comparison in the Kingdom of God, and we don't have to choose between either living a life of prayer and devotion, or serving—we are to choose both! So, whether in the past you've considered yourself a Mary, or a Martha, and making that determination has disqualified you from being in the other camp, the wall is now torn down, and the camp enlarged. It's time for Mary and Martha to come together. After all, they were sisters, and they did live in the same house. So should we!

BOWELS OF COMPASSION

We've looked at the Greek word for compassion previously, but it would be good to look again, perhaps more practically. Compassion literally means, "the bowels." The bowels are part of the intestinal tract, and though we don't like to talk about that part of our bodies, we do see an enlightening analogy here. In earlier times the bowels were considered to be the seat of pity, tenderness, and courage.

The bowels are the deepest parts of our bodies, the last stop within our digestive tracts. The food we eat goes through many different processes as it is absorbed by our digestive system, but where we receive the greatest nutrition from our food is as it passes through the bowels.

Similarly, we drink the pure milk of the Word of God (see 1 Peter 2:2), and we begin to digest its truths, that we might grow. However, we have to get it past our minds. We need to let it find its way into our hearts. It needs to go through every part of our "digestive" process, and if we stop short of the "bowels of compassion," we have missed the greatest release of spiritual nourishment and enrichment. If we listen, and take notes, and recite spiritual truth, but never act on it, or apply it, all that has happened is that our brains just got bigger, not our hearts!

Paul writes, *"Clothe yourselves therefore, as God's own chosen ones (His own picked representatives), [who are] purified and holy and well-beloved [by God Himself, by putting on behavior marked by] tenderhearted pity and mercy, kind feeling, a lowly opinion of yourselves, gentle ways, [and] patience [which is tireless and long-suffering, and has the power to endure whatever comes, with good temper]"* (Col. 3:12).

We must not only put off anger and wrath, but we must put on compassion and kindness. This is a decision we must make if we want to follow God's ways. It's a commitment we make to God.

I've had people come up to me at conferences and different gatherings, asking me to pray for them to receive an impartation for compassion. I've thought about this a lot, and I've come to the conclusion that I don't think that is possible. Just as our bodies process the food that causes the bowels to act, so should our spirits, as we process the love of God and His Word, bring our "bowels of compassion" to act. You can't eat food in the physical, and not have the process that brings elimination—you can't have one without the other. Compassion acts!

I've been concerned not only about the condition of my own heart, but also the heart of the Church. If we're having a difficult time getting this individually, then how can the Kingdom of God advance corporately? The answer is obvious—we can't.

I've had a thought come to me concerning all this. Once, when I was in a deep place in prayer, on the hard stone floor of the Elijah Inn in Pemba, Mozambique, I believe the Lord showed me something. As I lay there, while deep in a place of travail, intense heat, and all of our team groaning and laboring for God's justice to be established in the land, I saw the Body of Christ. I saw the call to have compassion and to act. But then I saw something else. The Body thought it was functioning well, and performing the will of God, but in actuality, it had no bowel! It did not even realize that it was missing a major body part—one of the most important organs where most of the nutrition comes from, that feeds and brings nourishment to all the other body parts. Of course, we need to pray—really pray that we get this, both individually and corporately. We need to pray for a miraculous release! The Lord has been showing different ones that there are rooms in Heaven that are full of body parts—waiting for a wave of unprecedented healing anointing to be released. Why not pray for supernatural release for the Body—a wave of unprecedented compassion across all lands, to all people groups, tribes, tongues and nations!

Charles Spurgeon wrote this about compassion: "It is expressive of the deepest emotion; a striving of the bowels—a yearning of the innermost nature with pity.... When our Savior looked upon certain sights, those who watched Him closely perceived that His internal agitation was very great, His emotions were very deep, and then His face betrayed it, His eyes gushed like founts with tears, and you saw that His big heart was ready to burst with pity for the sorrow upon which His eyes were gazing. His whole nature was agitated with commiseration for the sufferers before Him."[1]

Jesus Christ is a compassionate Friend to precious souls; His bowels yearn in mercy and pity for those in need. It was this mercy that brought Him from Heaven to earth, and it was this mercy that took Him to the Cross. His compassion brought Him to action—even dying on the Cross for our sins, that we would be forgiven, and have fellowship with the Father. His compassion brought action!

I want to take a moment right now, to act on something. How can we talk about compassion, and not make a place for you to receive the greatest act of compassion Jesus ever expressed. His love for His Father was so great, Jesus offered His life to be a sacrifice on our behalf. His blood was offered at the Cross, so that our blood, our life, would not be required. We have sinned and fallen short of the glory of God. If we believe that Jesus is the Son of God, and we repent of our sins, and confess Him before others, the blood of Jesus will cover us totally, completely, and forever. From that point on, as God looks on us, He doesn't see any of our shortcomings because all He sees is the blood of His Son!

Jesus loves you. God the Father loves you. To use a phrase of Graham Cooke, "You can't make Him love you any more, and you can't make Him love you any less." He loves you without reservation, just as you are, right now! That's who He is, and what He does. That is the focus of His compassion. He longs and groans for His house to be full, for His table to be full, and it won't be full unless you are there. He desires to draw you to Himself today, and to never be separated from you ever again. He has done it all for you and me.

All you have to do is say yes to Jesus! If you've never said yes to Him before, or maybe He's tugging on your heart in a fresh way, just talk with Him now. Tell him you love Him, you believe in Him, and you want to walk with Him. He will hear you and will answer your prayers.

Paul writes, *"I appeal to you therefore, brethren, and beg of you in view of [all] the mercies of God, to make a decisive dedication of your bodies [presenting all your members and faculties] as a living sacrifice, holy (devoted, consecrated) and well pleasing to God, which is your reasonable (rational, intelligent) service and spiritual worship"* (Rom. 12:1).

This is what is needed today: a decisive dedication of our lives as living sacrifices to God, and truly this is a reasonable service for us to offer in light of all His mercies to us.

THE WORLD WE LIVE IN

The world is literally screaming at us, desperate for help. According to recent studies, 75 percent of the world's population lives in poverty. Most of these people live in the Third World, or developing countries. The average annual gross income for individual workers in Western countries is $27,000. Contrast that with the rest of the world, where the average annual gross income is between $450.00 and $2,500.00 per person.[2] What a difference!

Approximately 50 percent of the world's population is female. Women and girls suffer more from poverty than men. Forty percent of the world's population consists of children. They are the ones who suffer more than all others. In fact, over one billion children are at risk today, and many have become actual victims of extreme poverty, homelessness, the loss of their parents, child labor, abuse, slavery, sexual exploitation, AIDS and other illnesses, and the effects of war and religious persecution.[3]

In certain parts of the world, orphaned children are conscripted into armies, and suffer sexual, mental, and physical abuse. They are forced to carry guns and trained to kill. At times, the governments involved are willing to "sell off" numbers of these children, to ease their financial situations. Finances are needed today for these purposes. I know of dear, precious saints who are working behind the lines to rescue these children and give them hope for their destiny and restore self-respect and esteem.

In just a few sentences we have been given a huge amount of information of which, if every one of us applied all our resources, strength and energy, could not begin to meet all these needs. Sometimes it can be quite easy to read the words, but not engage our hearts in the reality of what they mean. If those children were our children, or those people, our family, don't you think our attitude would be different? I know mine would! And yet, that is what the Lord wants to do; enlarge our hearts to such a degree that "they" become "our family." They are His kids, the love of His heart, and we just don't seem to get it or care. When will we get it? When will we engage, and do something about these needs?

If there ever was a time for compassion in our world, it is today!

THE DEBORAH COMPANY

There is a need for the Deborah anointing today. Judges 5:7 says, *"...until you arose—you, Deborah, arose—a mother in Israel!"* The conditions that Deborah and the Israelites were faced with were a complete disruption of the entire region. Judges 5:6-7 gives this description, *"After the days of Shamgar son of Anath, after the days of Jael* [meaning here Ehud] *the caravans ceased, travelers walked through byways. The villages were unoccupied and rulers ceased in Israel, until you arose...."*

There was no protection for the people. No laws were enforced. The people couldn't even travel on the roads, they had to sneak along hidden pathways, because the Philistine army was all about, raiding, killing, plundering their crops, their homes, their very existence. Then, Deborah arose!

The name Deborah, means "bee." Like a bee, Deborah was a very industrious woman. She judged Israel, but was particularly devoted to the reestablishment of true biblical worship in the temple. It is said that she spent time making the wicks for the candles that would be used in the temple. How appropriate this is when you realize that as Judges 4:4 mentions the word, Lapidoth, it is a Hebrew term that deals with light or illumination. Different translations give various meanings to this word. Deborah was either married to a man named Lapidoth, or she came from a region with that name. We see that Deborah, who served as a prophetess and judge in ancient Israel, was a bearer of great light, illumination, and wisdom.

Deborah was a very courageous woman who was not afraid to take risks. (See Judges 4.) While she was sitting under her palm tree, a symbol of authority from which she judged, in the hill country of Ephraim, the Israelites came up to her, bringing their grievances concerning the onslaught of attacks from the army of Jabin, the King of Canaan. Then she called for Barak, an army general and told him to go forth into battle and that God would give him victory over Sisera, the general who was commanding the Philistine army.

Barak responded to her prophecy by saying that he would go to the River Kishon, where the battle would take place, but he would do so only if she would agree to go with him. Deborah said, *"I will surely go with you; nevertheless, the trip you take will not be for your glory, for the Lord will sell Sisera into the hand of a woman…"* (Judg. 4:9).

What had Barak seen in Deborah's life that caused him to want her to go into warfare with him? What qualities did she possess that made him feel strengthened in her presence? Why would he ask a woman to take part in the battle with him?

I believe it's because he saw her as a woman of illumination, someone who walked in the light and glory of God. She was a wise, industrious, and brave woman who knew God. Therefore, I believe Barak was saying in effect, "I'm not going to go into battle unless you go with me, unless I have the illumination and presence of God with me."

Deborah had divine illumination and she had the presence of the Lord. Barak, also a prophet, had the administrative ability to raise an army and go out into the field and do the work.

Neither one could do without the other, and neither one cared who received the glory. They just wanted to defeat the enemy and to give all the glory to God. The result was: *"…Sisera lay dead, and the tent pin was in his temples. So God subdued on that day Jabin king of Canaan before the Israelites"* (Judg. 4:22-23). Commerce was restored, villages and families were restored, law and order was restored. When the government of God is set in place, it displaces all other governments.

I believe there is a new release of the Deborah anointing, but this time around it's not given to just one person, it's for a whole company of women who want to see the illumination of God and His Kingdom established, and are willing to become breakers in the Spirit—to break it open!

In a similar vein, I believe there is a whole company of Baraks, who don't care if the glory goes to men or women, they just want God to show up—that's all that matters. They are trustworthy and know how to wage war, and how to win.

WAR GENERALS

What we're talking about here is the Body of Christ coming into formation, becoming connected. In order for us to truly be effective in this battle for compassion, there has to be order, good supply lines, and good communication. I believe the Lord wants to release a whole army of compassionate warriors, and if there is to be a whole army, then there certainly has to be commanders overseeing, directing, and caring for the troops. We need to assemble ourselves together, and gather around those who are further down the road than we are—ones who are filled with courage, vision, and passion for God. These are men and women who are committed to defending the Gospel. They are not afraid of warfare, and they are eager to engage in all necessary battles, and are willing to fight.

God wants generals, or breakers, who know His heart. Unlike the world's concept of what a general looks like, God's generals are ones who know authority, yes; but they follow the example of their Master and Savior. They live their lives carrying a towel, ready to love and to serve. They know the meaning of the phrase, "lower still." They understand that the authority they carry comes from the greatest servant of all, Jesus!

He calls us to *"fight the good fight of faith"* (1 Tim. 6:12). With His help we will rise up as the army of God, replete with generals, majors, sergeants, corporals, and privates. We will be *"more than conquerors"* (Rom. 8:37), carrying our swords, our shields, and our towels.

I hear the sound of horses' hooves pounding the ground and the sounds of victory filling the air. The battle is the Lord's and through Him we will be victorious!

THE INNKEEPER ANOINTING

This battle has many fronts. There are some in particular that I feel the Lord is highlighting and sounding a fresh prophetic call. I believe He is releasing specific anointings to accomplish these assignments.

One of them is what I like to call, "The Innkeeper" anointing. Most of us are familiar with the parable of the Good Samaritan. (See Luke 10:30-35.) In this story we learn that a certain man had been robbed, stripped, wounded, and left to die. He was slighted by those who should have been his friends and helpers, including a priest who should have known better and a Levite who was supposed to show forth tenderness and compassion to those in need. When the Levite saw this man, he went over and took a close look at him, then crossed to the other side of the street when he saw the condition he was in. In other words, the Levite got as far away from him as he could.

Another man, a Samaritan, came along, and when he saw the injured man, he had compassion on him. Using his own linen, which he probably tore from his own clothing, he bound up the man's wounds. He poured oil and wine into the man's wounds and then put him on his own donkey. He took him to an inn, put him to bed, and paid the innkeeper for his accommodations.

Previously, I've focused on the Samaritan in this Scripture passage. While the Samaritan anointing is desperately needed and covers a wide range of compassionate acts, I want to acknowledge the innkeeper. He is barely mentioned, but he is also important. We need to have those who will go out into the streets and find the wounded ones, but there has to be some place to bring them in, for full restitution. The innkeeper already has his placement established, rooms available and ready, at a moment's notice. His would be like an extended care ministry. It may be in the form of recovery facilities—it could literally be families who will open up their homes.

This ministry is very practical, and could be very personal. Do you have an extra bedroom the Lord could use? Are you open for a

"Samaritan" to come into your life, and drop into your lap someone who needs help? This is one of the anointings that God is releasing among His people today. God wants us to provide for all those who are lying alongside the road in a state of hopelessness, despair, and great need. You don't know how much you have to offer until you see how deep the needs of these people are.

IMPACTING NATIONS

We need to ask for answers to questions the world has yet to ask. We need to look into the future, and ask the Lord for creative solutions and inventions. We need to look at ways to create entrepreneurial businesses to create jobs for those in low income areas, and help boost economies. We need to ask for houses, and look for ones that can be salvaged, repaired, and used for places of recovery or rescue.

How about a marriage of compassion with the prophetic? How about building relationships with our police, finding out the needs of our cities, and developing prophetic intercessory teams who will pray and ask for specific answers? We need to see what we can do to rescue and create a net to catch the women and children who have been trapped in sex trade businesses and prostitution, and are looking for a way out.

We need to develop water filtration systems that are inexpensive, easy to set up and establish in third world countries; and develop supply lines so ministries learn to work together and serve each other. We need to bring help in such a way that it releases blessing to whole areas. We need to cross over boundary lines of denominations and affiliations, reaching into areas that just plain need help. We need to move forward in Kingdom understandings and applications and build relationally and most importantly, in love.

We need to care for the poor and needy, the widow and orphan, not only within our own regions, but we need to have an international expression as well. Africa is dying right now! Our help is needed right now. They need simple things—beans and rice—by the trailer loads. Whole families are being lost. Here in the United States, most major cities are full of kids who have run away from home; they are living on the streets and taking drugs. These are our kids—these are our people. Jesus, open our eyes and hearts!

PREPARING OUR FIELDS

Being raised in rural Missouri from birth until James and I were married, I have a great appreciation for the parabolic language regarding nature and agriculture that is used in the Bible. I spent many, many hours in the hot sun with an ever aching back and sunburned arms, weeding our huge vegetable garden, harvesting those vegetables and preparing and storing them. We kept the kitchen stove running for days at a time, canning beans, tomatoes, and various fruits. We processed countless chickens, cutting them up and freezing them. We processed cherries, peaches, apples, pears, raspberries, and plums.

We spent whole days at my grandmother's house fighting our way through endless blackberry thickets, actually creating tunnels through the tangled maze of thorny canes, and coming home with tubs and tubs full to put in the freezer. I've worked out in the hayfields with my brothers, running the tractor so they could pick up the bales and stack them on the wagon. That hay was necessary for our cattle to make it through the winter. I've known the necessity and value of tending plants, tending gardens and fields.

> *And when you reap the harvest of your land, you shall not reap your field to its very corners, neither shall you gather the fallen ears or gleanings of your harvest. And you shall not glean your vineyard bare, neither shall you gather its fallen grapes: you shall leave them for the poor and the stranger. I am the Lord your God* (Leviticus 19:9-10).

I believe the Lord is issuing a challenge to us, for we all have "fields" that we are laboring in, fields the Lord has given to us. It's in these fields that we must plant the seeds that will bring forth a bountiful harvest. Everyone has a sphere of influence; it may be your work place, it may be your home, it may be the school you attend, it may be your ethnic background, or the region where you live.

We must prepare our fields in such a way that we allow the poor and the strangers to benefit from the harvest. The times in which we live make this a very urgent matter, for we see a great increase in natural disasters, terrorism, war, and disease around the globe.

Plant good seed in your field, and be sure to plant what God tells you to plant. While you do so, make certain that you leave some fruit in your field so that the poor can reap some from your harvest, too.

REST AND REJOICE

The seventh year was meant to be a year of rest and rejoicing. The Bible says, *"But the seventh year you shall release it and let it rest and lie fallow, that the poor of your people may eat* [what the land voluntarily yields], *and what they leave the wild beasts shall eat. In like manner you shall deal with your vineyard and olive grove"* (Exod. 23:11).

As we get to know the heart of God, we need to get our lives in line with His calendar. The seventh year represents perfection and completion, a fulfillment of the will of God, which demands that the land should lie fallow so the poor can reap a benefit, and so the land can rest.

The seventh year was a year of breakthrough and blessing both for the landowners and the poor. Everyone shared in the good things God had provided for them.

In the Book of Esther we read: *"As the days on which the Jews got rest from their enemies, and as the month which was turned for them from sorrow to gladness and from **mourning into a holiday**—that they should make them days of feasting and gladness, days of sending choice portions to one another and gifts to the poor"* (Esther 9:22, emphasis mine).

We need to enlarge our hearts to include the poor as part of our times of celebration. Remember too, that when deliverance, in whatever form it may take, comes to your house, that as you enter into celebration God's heart is that you remember the poor. Let your deliverance spill over to those who are still waiting for their own deliverance to be released.

We have looked at compassion and the heart of God from many different angles. We have now come to the culmination of these many pages. Now is the moment of decision. Time is an intriguing element. We have a past, and we speak of a future. But where both become a reality is right now. In reality, now is all that we have. We can do nothing about our past, but if we act now, we can establish what will become our past. We can talk about the future, but the problem is, the future is always ahead of us, we can never live in the future.

We must live in the *now*. If we try to live in the future, we're always dreaming, and never realizing. We need to take our dreams, and make practical steps today to see them come to pass. We need to move out of any remorse over past mistakes or missed opportunities, and make a decision to get up and act now!

THE POOR MAN'S WATCH

When preparing to go on my first trip to Mozambique to serve Iris Ministries with Rolland and Heidi Baker, I bought a simple plastic watch. It was very cheap, but it actually had more bells and whistles than my nicer watch, and was a great tool for the trip. When I got home, I unpacked my clothes, developed my pictures, gave out gifts to my loved ones, and tried to "get my life in order again." There was my nice pretty watch laying on my nightstand, waiting for me to take it up again, but something inside me didn't want to put it back on. Days went by, weeks went by, and I just couldn't take this simple cheap little watch off my wrist.

I went to the Lord, asking Him what was going on—didn't I want to go forward, was I holding onto something I needed to release? Finally one day my friend, precious Holy Spirit spoke to me. He said, "You are on the poor man's watch." This word went through my heart like an arrow. I knew it to be true. There was no taking it off—there was no "getting my life back in order." In actuality, my life was getting in God's order.

God has a poor man's watch that is perfect for each one of us. It is not a gift, it's part of the Kingdom of God. If we want to experience His Kingdom, we have to wear the watch.

NEXT TIME JESUS WILL COME

I have a promise from Jesus. A number of years ago, I had an angelic visitation that lasted several weeks. It was awesome, wonderful, fearful, unsettling, challenging, and life altering. Toward the end of this visitation, I was talking with God, telling Him I didn't want this to end. I was lovesick, and I didn't want to go back to life as I knew it before. My heart had been touched and transformed by being in His presence. In the quiet early morning hours, before the sun had even thought of rising, Holy Spirit spoke to me. He said, "Next time, not only will the angels come, but Jesus Himself will come."

LOOKING FOR JESUS

I'm looking for Jesus; I'm waiting for Jesus. But could it be that Jesus is waiting for me? Could it be that as I engage my heart to not only hear the Word of God, but to live the Word to those who do not know Him, Jesus just might come to me? That sounds like the Kingdom of God coming on the earth! I want to be a part of establishing God's Kingdom, and raising up a whole army of like-hearted loving warriors who have embraced the call to compassion. He is waiting for you. Will you enlist in this army? I pray that your answer is yes, and that you are stirred to action—because compassion acts!

> *Dear Lord Jesus, I come to you this day, volunteering myself to be your arms, your feet, your hands to hurting and needy people. I want to embrace your heart for the poor, the orphan and the widow. I want to offer to you the field you have given me, that you would show me how to help provide for those who are less fortunate. Lord, I ask you to speak to me, lead me into the avenues of service that I am to engage in. Lord, according to James 1:5, give me the wisdom I need to move forward, connect with the people I need to network with. Today I make a commitment in my heart, with my mouth, to show You and the world my faith, by my works—because I love you, and I know that You so love me! In Jesus Name, Amen!*

ENDNOTES

1. Wesley Campbell and Stephen Court, *Be A Hero: The Battle for Mercy and Social Justice* (Destiny Image, 2004), 165.

2. Ibid., 165-168.

3. http://www.hrw.org/press/2002/10/burma-1016.htm.

RESOURCES &
CONTACT
INFORMATION

D r. James W. and Michal Ann Goll are the cofounders of Encounters Network—Ministry to the Nations. They are members of the Harvest International Ministries Apostolic Team and contributing writers for *Kairos* magazine and other periodicals. James and Michal Ann have four children and live in the beautiful rolling hills of Franklin, Tennessee. They have produced numerous study guides on subjects such as *Equipping in the Prophetic, Blueprints for Prayer,* and *Empowered for Ministry,* all available through the Encounters Resource Center.

For more information contact:

ENCOUNTERS NETWORK

PO Box 1653

Franklin, TN 37075

Office phone: 615-599-5552

Office fax: 615-599-5554

For orders call: 1-877-200-1604

For more information or to sign up for monthly e-mail communiqués, visit their website at www.encountersnetwork.com or e-mail: info@encountersnetwork.com.

Other books by James W. and Michal Ann Goll:

Fire On the Altar

The Lost Art of Intercession

Kneeling on the Promises

Wasted on Jesus

Exodus Cry

Elijah's Revolution

The Coming Prophetic Revolution

Women on the Front Lines—A Call to Courage

A Call to the Secret Place

Intercession

The Beginner's Guide to Hearing God

The Seer

God Encounters

Praying for Israel's Destiny

The Seer Devotional Journal

The Lost Art of Practicing His Presence

Dream Language

The Prophetic Intercessor

Angelic Encounters

Compassion Acts

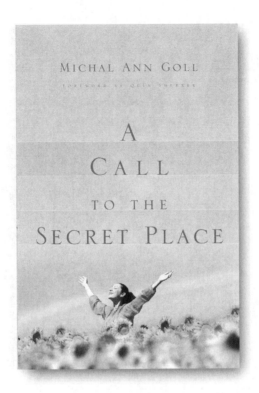

A CALL TO THE SECRET PLACE

Deep inside each one of us is a longing to escape the frantic pace of life in the 21st Century. *A Call to the Secret Place* is your personal invitation to take that step toward the place lovingly prepared for you. Cheering you on will be the voices of other women as shared by Michal Ann Goll like Madam Guyon, Susanna Wesley, Fanny Crosby, Basilea Schlink, Gwen Shaw, Beth Alves and others. Their collective voices call out inviting you to join them in the privacy of a loving moment with your Lord.

ISBN 0-7684-2179-9

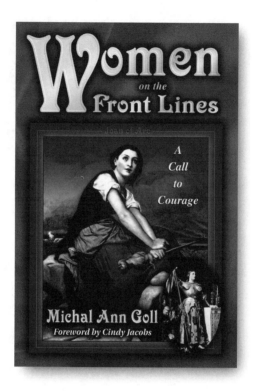

WOMEN ON THE FRONT LINE SERIES
A CALL TO COURAGE

History is filled with ordinary women who have changed the course of their generation. Here, Michal Ann Goll, co-founder of Ministry to the Nations with her husband Jim, shares how her own life was transformed and highlights nine women whose lives will impact yours! Every generation faces the same choices and issues; learn how you, too, can heed the call to courage and impact a generation.

ISBN 0-7684-2020-2

Study Guides by James W. Goll

Over the years, James W. Goll has taught these practical tools to help people all over the world learn a prophetic lifestyle. The comprehensive study guides in this series can be used either for individual study or with a class or small group. Following each detailed lesson are simple questions for reflection. As you work through these lessons, you will be inspired to take your place in God's prophetic army.

Blueprints for Prayer Prelude To Revival

Consecrated Contemplative Prayer
This study guide offers insight into truths discovered by Christian mystics of the past. Chapters include "Ministry Of Fasting", "Contemplative Prayer", and "Quieting Our Souls Before God". Great for developing communion with God.

$15.00

Watchman on the Walls
These twelve lessons are great for personal use, prayer groups, sermons or Bible studies. Lessons include "Fire On The Altar", "Christ Our Priestly Model", "The Watch Of The Lord", "From Prayer to His Presence", "Identification in Intercession", and more.

$15.00

Strategies of Intercession
These twelve detailed lessons include the following subjects: "Confessing Generational Sins", "Praying for Those in Authority", and "Praying on Site with Insight". Thorough and precise, this study guide will expose you to the many different strategies and models of prayer.
$15.00

Compassionate Prophetic Intercession
In this study guide you will find twelve detailed lessons on the folling topics: "Travail: The Prayer that Brings Birth", "Prophetic Intercession", "Praying Down Supernatural Encounters", "Wisdom Issues for Intercessors", and more.
$15.00

www.jamesgoll.com or Call 1~877~200~1604

Study Guides by James W. Goll

Over the years, James W. Goll has taught these practical tools to help people all over the world learn a prophetic lifestyle. The comprehensive study guides in this series can be used either for individual study or with a class or small group. Following each detailed lesson are simple questions for reflection. As you work through these lessons, you will be inspired to take your place in God's prophetic army.

Equipping in the Prophetic | Enlisting a Prophetic Army

Prophetic Foundations

The first of this series on the prophetic. These 12 lessons include:
For the Many - Not the Few, The History of the Prophetic,
Intimacy in the Prophetic, Power & Perils of the Prophetic Spirit
Seven Expressions of the Prophetic Spirit, Prophesy Life,
The Prophetic Song of the Lord, and more...

$15.00

Experiencing Dreams & Visions

This is the second Guide in the series. These 12 lessons include:
God's Multi-faceted Voice, Visionary Revelation, Journaling,
Tools For Interpreting Revelation, Dream Language,
Receiving and Judging Revelation, Wisdom in Handling Revelation,
Dream Language I & II, Tips for Interpratations , and more...

$15.00

Prophetic Maturation

This is the third Guide in the series. These 12 lessons Include:
Called Into Character, From Character to Commissioning,
Seizing your Prophetic Destiny Parts 1 & 2, The Cross -
The Prophetic Lifestyle, Four levels of Prophetic Ministry,
The Seer and the Prophet: Similarities and Differences, and more...

$15.00

Understanding Supernatural Encounters

This is the fourth Guide in the series. These 12 lessons Include:
Keys to the Supernatural, How to Receive Revelation,
Demonstrating Three Models, The Deception of the Anointing,
Levels Of Supernatural Visions Parts 1 & 2, Trances Defined,
Ministry and Function of Angels, Current Day Accounts of Angelic
Activity, and more...

$15.00

Dream Language Resources by James W. & Michal Ann Goll

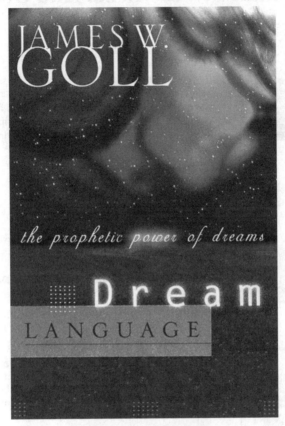

Book $15.00
*13 CD Set $80.00
*13 Session DVD Set $110.00
Dream Language Study Guide $15.00

*CD & DVD Sessions were recorded live as James and Michal Ann taught this class.

**For these Products and Additional Products
by James W. and Michal Ann Goll
please visit our web site or call 1-877-200-1604**

Visit www.encountersnetwork.com

Additional Resources by
James W. & Michal Ann Goll

Prophetic Encounters

Featuring James W. Goll
Music by John Belt
Be prepared to receive a Prophetic Encounter as James W. Goll shares stories, and personal experiences, reads scripture and releases prayers of impartation. Titles include: Beautiful, Bread of His Presence, Rock the Nations, Over Here, Dread Champions, Giants of Faith, Days of Acceleration, The Golden Anointing, and many more...

$15.00

The Healing Presence

Featuring James W. & Michal Ann Goll
Music by John Belt
Receive God's Healing Presence as James W. & Michal Ann Goll read scripture, share stories, and release prayers of impartation. "The Lord really visited us in this recording!"
Titles include: The Hem of His Garment, The Day of Healing, How Lovely, The Healing River, and many more...

$15.00

Invitation To Intimacy

This CD was professionally recorded at the Wagner Leadership Institute as James W. Goll was caught up into another realm. It contains over 60 minutes of prophetic, spontaneous worship and teaching with keyboard and instrumentation with John Belt. Soak with this one!

$15.00

Sacred Fire

by John Belt
This non-stop instrumental CD will take you on a journey with many creative sounds. The sacred fire is fire that burns in our lives before God in prayer. Songs include Waters of Moriah, Sacred Fire, Celestial Door, Heaven's Shores and others . . .

$15.00

For Additional Products by James W. and Michal Ann Goll
Visit www.jamesgoll.com | Call 1~877~200~1604

Thoughts and Reflections

Thoughts and Reflections

Thoughts and Reflections

Thoughts and Reflections

Thoughts and Reflections

Thoughts and Reflections

Thoughts and Reflections

Thoughts and Reflections

Thoughts and Reflections

Thoughts and Reflections

Thoughts and Reflections

Additional copies of this book and other
book titles from DESTINY IMAGE are
available at your local bookstore.

For a bookstore near you, call 1-800-722-6774.

Send a request for a catalog to:

Destiny Image₀ Publishers, Inc.
P.O. Box 310
Shippensburg, PA 17257-0310

*"Speaking to the Purposes of God for this
Generation and for the Generations to Come."*

For a complete list of our titles,
visit us at www.destinyimage.com